VERMONT ~~~~~~ COLLEGE
MONTPELIER, VT.

WITHDRAWN

WITHDRAWN

THE
WEDDING
BOOK

WITHDRAWN

THE
WEDDING
BOOK

A Complete His and Her Guide

By FRANCES and FREDERIC A. BIRMINGHAM

HARPER & ROW, PUBLISHERS

NEW YORK, EVANSTON, AND LONDON

Illustrated by Jon Buelow

THE WEDDING BOOK. Copyright © 1964 by Frances and Frederic A. Birmingham. Printed in the United States of America. All rights reserved. No part of this book may be used or reproduced in any manner whatsoever without written permission except in the case of brief quotations embodied in critical articles and reviews. For information address Harper & Row, Publishers, Incorporated, 49 East 33rd Street, New York 16, N.Y.

FIRST EDITION

LIBRARY OF CONGRESS CATALOG CARD NUMBER: 63:10626

395.2
B619w

Contents

--◦❈{ v }❈◦--

14352

CONTENTS

CONTENTS

Acknowledgments

ALL BOOKS ARE DRAWN from life experience in some degree and all authors are conscious of shadowy contributors standing distantly behind the words. This book more than most owes its meaning to a host of friends and advisors who have knowingly or unwittingly contributed to the ideas and information we have set down here. Any author setting out to define marriage custom must be an ancient mariner upon uncharted seas and he stoppeth one of three out of every wedding party he encounters for the correct advice. We have in our time stopped so many hostesses, clergymen, members of bridal parties, and authorities in many fields, that we must thank them as a host of helpers, with affection and appreciation. We owe a special debt to our friend Mr. Morton Minsky, for his wise counsel and assistance throughout our work; to Mr. Ken White, who cracked the whip, but never quite applied it; to Mr. Jon Buelow, who illustrated the book with such taste and gentle wit under conditions of distracting pressure; and to Mrs. Rosada Gonzales, who sweetly, patiently, and efficiently brought law and order unto a tortured manuscript seemingly composed of archaic fragments of Urdu, Sanskrit, and cuneiform handwriting. In addition, we wish to acknowledge especially the source material provided by the following arbiters in each field, establishing an impeccable background of authority and assurance which is passed along to the young couples who will read this book as one of the finest gifts of the happy occasion: Mr. Meyer Davis, America's leading purveyor of music; Miss Irene Hayes, New York's foremost originator in flower design; Miss Candy Jones, director of her own success school for young ladies, and the personal embodiment of glamor and poise; as well as the outstanding organizations representing the finest products and services in the world, the Waldorf-Astoria Hotel and its renowned cuisine; W. & J. Sloane, Inc., internationally famous for decor; Tiffany & Co., a synonym for illustriousness in jewelry, silver, china, and crystal; Thomas Cook & Son, known around the world for helping people get around the world; and to The Diamond Sales Corporation, for various basic information and statistics.

The information with reference to laws on the issuance of marriage licenses, given on page 54, is based upon statistics compiled by the Council on Marriage Relations, Inc., New York City, and appears through the courtesy of *The World Almanac and Book of Facts,* Copyright 1964 by New York World-Telegram Corporation.

Preface

GETTING MARRIED is a favorite sport in the United States.

Last June the *New York Times* announced 230 engagements and 650 weddings in that month alone.

In the last year of record, there were 1,547,000 marriages filed in the United States.

Yet, for all this, we had noticed that there is no Baedeker of the bridal ceremony, no rulebook for star-crossed lovers who need a guide. Of course, there are official marriage counselors, specialists on the staffs of department stores, magazines devoted entirely or seasonally to the subject, and beyond these competent people a horde of unruly characters filled with rules you must follow or sacrifice their affections. But not one of these good people can you take by the hand, close a door, and consult in privacy as with a helpmate-to-be. There are a few excellent volumes in the bookstores, as far as they go. But none of them pays much attention to that forgotten man, the groom, and they are uniformly joyless in the face of the happiest occasion of all.

So we decided to write one that was informal in approach and formal in authority. We had enough personal experience to rely on: Fran had been a member of at least seven bridal parties before her own, and Fred had been a best man three times in one summer, and ushered his way successfully through many a tour of duty before sitting at the head of the table at his own bachelor dinner.

Ours was a large wedding, and Fran had her picture in the New York papers and in those of her home town, Scranton, Pennsylvania. It had all the trimmings, and we had the best time of our lives. We tried hard to avoid any improvisations which might provide unscheduled merriment for the guests, but we didn't quite succeed.

We had heard of several inspirations that had gone awry. Candy Jones told us of a girl who had secretly ordered the church organist to play at an important moment the ballad known to her and her groom as "our song." The trouble was, that when those lovely strains soared out over the church not only the groom but the hundreds of guests found a hilarious interpretation in the song that the romantic-minded girl hadn't even dreamed of. But she should have: the song was "Love for Sale."

And then there was the bride, very proud of her voice, who turned to her groom in the middle of the ceremony, looked him straight in the eye, and let him have it with "Oh, Promise Me," full volume. He recoiled, and it was the opinion of many of those present that if the best man hadn't restrained him bodily, he'd still be running.

Brides aren't always to blame, though; with us it was the groom. Fred had come to the wedding in Scranton from New York City and he thought he had packed everything. And so he had—everything but his shoes. Now, he is a big guy, and big guys have big feet. Scranton was combed for a pair of black, formal 11½'s, and Fred could find just one pair. Modestly priced, on sale. Good. The wedding was in a Presbyterian church, but in honor of the fact that the groom was a wayward Episcopalian, Fran's mother sweetly decided to provide a white *prie-dieu,* so that the couple might kneel for the blessing at the end of the ceremony, an innovation for Presbyterians. It was a fine gesture, indeed, marred only by the fact that when the groom knelt, on the bottom of one generously proportioned shoe it said SALE and on the other $3.98. Elegantly as he had garbed himself, it was clear for all to see that he was a cheap skate who haunted bargain basements even for shoes to get married in. All the guests agreed that Fran was in for a tightwad life with *him!*

There was still another slip, more happily concluded. Fred had bought some beautiful black pearl stickpins for his best man and ushers to wear, but they were stolen on the trip up. He dashed around town trying to replace them, on his shoe hegira, but there were none to be had. But while buying some of his flowers (see page 73 for just what the groom is responsible for in the way of flowers), he had an inspiration. The florist had some simulated black pearl corsage pins—quite long, a dusty gray, but with the "pearl" swirled, probably done at the time the pins were originally dipped into some plastic goo at the corsage-pin factory. Fred invested in them: they were ten cents for a dozen. The boys wore them bravely, and the pins were a howling success. The leading socialite in the community, a lady of great means, confided to one of the ushers that those "swirly pearls" were the most beautiful she had ever seen.

Otherwise, all went well, and the party that followed was such a tremendous success that we didn't want to leave at all and only did so when shooed out for the sake of some elderly guests who were getting sleepy.

It was a great event, our greatest.

And so we want yours to be.

And so we wrote this book.

And open it with a toast: "Lifelong happiness to you, our favorite bride and groom."

FRANCES AND FREDERIC A. BIRMINGHAM

Dobbs Ferry, New York

My true-love hath my heart, and I have his,
  By just exchange one for the other given:
I hold his dear, and mine he cannot miss;
  There never was a better bargain driven:
His heart in me keeps him and me in one,
  My heart in him his thoughts and senses guides:
He loves my heart, for once it was his own,
  I cherish his, because in me it bides . . .

  My true-love hath my heart, and I have his.

SIR PHILIP SIDNEY

Chapter One

It Happens in the Best Families

IT IS NO NEWS to the young that love is the most powerful force in the universe.

Once upon a time a man looked down at what he had wrought and mused, "I have created a weapon so terrible that it will outlaw war." In his hands he held a bow and arrow.

So much for the heavy thinkers. Today they can send a man into outer space, and perhaps to another planet. But all of them—thinkers, astronauts, builders, destroyers—have no answer to the look in the eyes of a girl, or what it does to their own hearts. Wars have been fought, kingdoms won and lost, for love; and that is the way it always will be, whether power is measured in the blow of a club or a hydrogen bomb. Against love, power itself is a mere toy.

Fortunately for us all, the skeins of love and its consequences are our most ancient and treasured tradition. Nothing in our lives today, whether science, literature, language, history, or the nations themselves, reaches as far back into our civilization as the customs of marriage.

Love has always found a language for itself in flowers. A South Sea Island lad still says it with flowers—a white one draped over his right ear means that he's looking, a red hibiscus says that he's found her, while green leaves call the whole thing off. Algerians traditionally used bouquets, arranged in various flower patterns, to speak their messages of love. In Swiss villages the young man slips a love note

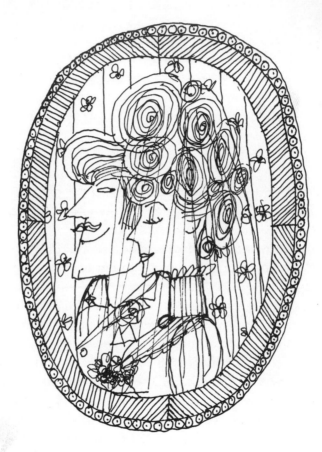

into a flowerpot and leaves it on the girl's windowsill. If she reads the note and takes the pot inside, he's won her, but he's out in the cold if the flowerpot is.

The inevitability of love has always been a favorite theme of poets. Sir Walter Scott sang:

> True love's the gift which God has given
> To man alone beneath the heaven . . .
> It is the secret sympathy,
> The silver link, the silken tie,
> Which heart to heart and mind to mind
> In body and in soul can bind.

In so saying, Sir Walter was by no means distant from an ancient Chinese belief that the old deity, Yue-laou, the old man of the moon, unites predestined couples together with a silken cord, after which nothing can affect their eventual coming together. Somewhat more briskly, an old English proverb puts it, "Hanging and marriage go by destiny."

The very symbol of our marriage ceremony, the ring, has the most charming traditions of all. Before its appearance, a love charm was used to soften a maiden's heart. Tristan and Isolde themselves drank a love potion. Others have downed heady cocktails of perfume, honey, poppy, and mistletoe. Even a carrot and-lettuce salad was once thought efficacious, and tomatoes are still called "love apples" in some rural parts of our own country. But the ring finally came into its own as a means of announcing the happy union.

The Anglo-Saxons were the first. They were betrothed as very young girls and boys and a pledge given for the future in the form of a ring, the symbol of eternity. The bridegroom-to-be placed on the maiden's right hand a ring, giving at the same time his pledge or "wed" (hence our term "wedding"), and she wore it for all to see, until the wedding itself. It was then transferred to her left hand, and the bridegroom slipped it symbolically upon each of her fingers in turn, naming as he did so the Holy Trinity, with an "Amen" for the fourth finger.

The fourth finger of the left hand was selected as the ring finger in the belief that a vein in the finger ran directly to the heart. For this reason, and also because it was the most protected and least used finger, this became the traditional bearer.

There was a charming custom in old England, that of the "geminal

--- { 5 } ---

ring," something so appealing to us today that it should really be revived. A double ring was cast, hinged so that it was really one, and sized so that one part could fit into the other, thus making it one in its original form. At a betrothal, the hinge was broken, and each kept a ring to wear as a pledge until the wedding. Sometimes there was a third ring on the same hinge, which a witness to the ceremony wore thereafter. The rings were often quite beautiful, of gold or silver, and imbedded with jewels. This custom lasted well into Elizabethan times, so that, even in certain versions of *Midsummer Night's Dream*, Helena could say:

> And I have found Demetrius like a gemmel
> Mine own, and not mine own.

Just as old a custom, and one still surviving, is that of baking a ring right into the wedding cake. This was also done with wedding drinks —the one who found it in the potion was slated to be wed.

The shoe became a member of the wedding in a curious way. At first it was a symbol of authority. In the Anglo-Saxon ceremony, after the groom had placed the ring on his bride's finger, her father then presented him with one of the girl's shoes, and the young man then gave her a clout on the head with it, as a sign that the law of the house had now passed from father to husband.

In another phase the groom sometimes kicked the bride as a symbol of his authority. As time went on, however, the shoe began to lose its meaning, but never its place. Eventually, it became more of a symbol of good luck than of household authority. In many ceremonies the wedding guests would line up—unmarried women here, unmarried men there—and the bride would fling the oldest and most battered shoe obtainable (preferably one purchased or stolen from an old tramp) to the girls. The lucky lass who caught it would without doubt be married within the year. This was the origin of the throwing of the bride's bouquet, which we still practice. In the original, however, the happy catcher of the shoe then flung it at the group of men: the one she hit was the one she would marry.

So the shoe has now outlived the phrase "and obey" in the marriage ceremony, which it originally emphasized. Domestic authority, it would seem, just ain't what it used to be.

In one ancient ceremony of a simpler day, the wife presented her husband with a special whip, made by her own itty-bitty hands, and an old Welsh law permitted a husband to chastise his wife on any part of her person except her head with three blows of a broomstick —provided that the stick be "not longer than his arm, nor thicker than his middle finger."

It was rough on the bride in those days. But at least she got a break once in a while. For instance, when Rolf married King Erik's daughter in ancient Scandinavia, she was provided with a shield, sword, and ax as part of her wedding outfit, just in case she found it necessary to defend herself from her husband's blows.

Sportsmen will appreciate the *joie de vivre* of a wedding custom in certain rustic areas of England, where a football was placed outside the church, and the bride, as she and the groom emerged, gave the ball a mighty root with her foot, thus symbolizing again the shoe bit about authority, and kicking off a mighty football game for the guests, all in one gesture.

Another rather sporty custom was followed in Scotland and called "creeling." On the day after the marriage, a group of friends called on the happy pair, and affixed a basket, or "creel," on the husband's back. It was then filled with rocks. It became his obligation to make a tour of the town at a dead run with this load, and he could only be relieved of his task by having his wife overtake him and free him with a kiss. Sometimes wives were too bashful to do this, or perhaps too mischievous, so that the groom's creeling was a strenuous experience. They no longer do it in Galashiels, however, ever since one Robert Young, using the excuse of "a sore back," failed to get out of bed at all on the day after his wedding, much less scamper about with rocks on his back. Perhaps the fact that he had been married twice before had something to do with this. Creeling was no novelty to Bob Young.

Community pranks of this nature have taken all sorts of forms. Bachelors were very unpopular in the Hellenic civilization and were

compelled to walk nude through the forum at least once a year, singing a scurrilous song about themselves. Marriages between the oddly
assorted—the very old to the very young, or perhaps involving widows
or widowers—have been somewhat cruelly celebrated in the past.
That was the origin of the charivari, actually a mock serenade of
discordant noises made on kettles and tin horns, designed to dismay
and insult the unfortunate pair. The custom has come down to our
own day in a much more good-humored form. Newly married couples,
particularly in rural areas, are often kept awake on their wedding
night by merrymakers serenading them until dawn, frequently with
a generous tattoo of pistols and other weapons being fired in the general exuberance.

It must be admitted that getting married in ancient times offered
a great many more hazards than it does today, involving some handy
work with horses and weapons.

Some nations were vigorous in their marriage customs. In the East
Indian Archipelago, a model husband-to-be was expected to look about
him before his marriage and then to cut off a number of heads in the
family group about him, in order to make room for the expected progeny
from the happy event. This was not as untidy as it might seem, at
least to their way of thinking, since they were all headhunters and
the noggins of the deceased relatives added substantially to the family
collection while simultaneously cutting down on the crowding.

No less realistic, a Scythian with an eye to the future would not
think of marrying a maiden who had not personally killed at least
one enemy and thus demonstrated her capacity to contribute to the
future welfare of the tribe.

Almost all of our remaining wedding customs—the "best man," the
carrying of the bride over the threshold, and the honeymoon—go back
to a process best described as stealing a wife.

(In a great many civilizations, as we know, a wife may be purchased, but good manners and good taste have always kept this type
of courtship out of polite family volumes such as this, lest evil-minded
persons make invidious comparisons with modern custom.)

Wife snatching was a high art in aboriginal Australia. There it was customary for any man wishing a girl for his wife simply to order her to follow him. If she didn't, he flung a spear at her. As a result, the prettiest girls on the island were marked and scarred by the furrows of many wounds, and never were quite able to settle down very long in one place. Clubbing the loved one insensible was also considered acceptable marriage etiquette. But the groom in this case had to prove himself worthy of his bride, particularly if he had hijacked her from some other warrior. As his test of character, he was attacked at a range of forty yards by ten other fighters of his tribe. Each one flung three spears, and he had as his only protection a bark shield about a foot square. If he survived, he qualified as a groom.

The Scandinavians, in their early history, stole their brides in an exceptionally canny way. They never swiped just any old girl. They waited until she had been decked out in her finery, was loaded down with all her gifts, and was on the way to the ceremony before they struck. Thus assured that she was wholly desirable, and thus having avoided the tedium of testing these matters beforehand, the predatory young man and his friends attacked the wedding procession. The bride was stoutly defended, of course, by the groom and his "best men." The phrase, you see, had real meaning in those days, when it took a corps of your huskiest friends to make sure that you wound up a wedding procession with your wife still included. There are still in Swedish museums examples of a curious kind of spear that had sockets in it for torches—weddings were best held at night in those days, and the "best men" wanted to see as well as thrust.

As less barbarous customs were reluctantly accepted into the family of so-called civilized nations, the pageant of marriage by capture was never wholly abandoned, at least as a symbol. In many nations, while giving up the idea of killing the bride's family and kinsmen simply in order to wed her, the custom of mock abduction still persists. The groom overtakes his bride in procession and rides away with her, with only token resistance on the part of her following. She, of course, bites, kicks, and scratches, because the idea of reluctance to marry has always seemingly been tied in with the virtues of modesty and chastity.

In rustic England they pelt the groom and his friends riding through town on the way to call for the bride, and swing sandbags over the girl's front door to unseat the horsemen if possible, or fire pistols in their general direction as they near the quarry.

Primitive? Perhaps. But thus do we today allow the groom a "best man." Thus, the groom takes her on a honeymoon: a delightful time of pristine wedded bliss away from prying eyes, but actually a throwback to his taking her to a hideaway after the theft and returning to his community only after the excitement had died down and the bride was indubitably his own. And still today, he carries her over the threshold into their first home, symbolizing the ancient theft by force. And, you know, it is still a stimulating gesture of masculine prowess-in-arms, particularly if the bride is buxom as well as beautiful.

Old as the human race, almost, is the bride's veil, to keep her modestly hidden from the gaze of any but her beloved before their marriage: and so she lifts it in the part of our own ceremony when she is most truly pronounced his wife.

And last, of course, the rice is thrown. As they have also thrown rye, oats, barley, beans, and corn. It is the age-old wish that the union may be blessed with a happy family.

These are some of the quaint and charming customs we have inherited from all the world, and taken as our own in many cases. Even the most practical of us must succumb to their allure at a time when true love has its greatest recognition. An old book tells us that "in Derbyshire, Wilshire and Oxfordshire, the bees always expected to be informed of a wedding and to have their hives decorated with a favor."

That is in a certain sense the reason for this book. For a wedding turns out to be for almost everyone. The bride's dilemma and decision really come down "to bee or not to bee." Who must be informed? Who must be decorated with a favor?

Tradition has decreed it all.

Let us look into this most happy custom.

How do I love thee? Let me count the ways.
I love thee to the depth and breadth and height
My soul can reach, when feeling out of sight
For the ends of Being and ideal Grace.
I love thee to the level of every day's
Most quiet need, by sun and candle-light.
I love thee freely, as men strive for Right;
I love thee purely, as they turn from Praise.
I love thee with the passion put to use
In my old griefs, and with my childhood's faith.
I love thee with a love I seemed to lose
With my lost saints—I love thee with the breath,
Smiles, tears, of all my life!—and, if God choose,
I shall but love thee better after death.

ELIZABETH BARRETT BROWNING

Chapter Two

🌹

An Engaging Custom

When captain miles standish lost the hand of his beloved Priscilla, simply because he lacked moral courage, and hired stand-in John Alden to pop the question, he was only getting what he deserved.

For this is a manly moment, this declaration of love's intention. It deserves some searching thought as to the doing as well as to the permanence of the affections behind it. That's why he should be in full control of everything, especially of himself, when

He pops the question

Fortunately for most males, there is no Sadie Hawkins Day in real life, when the slowest runners and the unwary may be overtaken or trapped into matrimony. Popping the question is still the male prerogative. There have been times, it is true, when the girl—sensing that the boy is shy or needs just a tiny push to put him over the edge —has helped matters along in one way or another. But a direct proposal by the girl not only implies that she intends to run things which belong in the masculine realm by tradition, but also that she suspects that the boy either is incapable of making up his own mind or has reached a negative conclusion. Either way, by speaking out she puts him in the uncomfortable position of accepting because he hasn't the nerve to get out of it. In any case, she is unthinking, ungallant, unmannered, unfeminine, and downright ungentlewomanly. Let's have none of it.

On the other hand, you must make careful plans for your own declaration and be prepared to carry it off with great elan and style if accepted, and with dignity and kindness if rejected.

To do so, you should examine in advance all alternatives. Let us start with the happiest, and most probable one—that she will say yes.

Girls are romantic, and this should be one of the unforgettable moments of their lives. Therefore you should try to pop the question under auspices worth remembering. You two could be dining in an especially beautiful or favorite spot, possibly connected with your first meeting or the dawning of your affection for each other. You might be walking together in the woods, looking at a timeless view of countryside or sea, driving under a benign moon, or riding across a sunny patch of countryside made especially for lovers. The memory of this scene, wherever it may be, will be a treasured one all your lives. And it will tell her also—as a sudden, seemingly unanticipated proposal can never do—that this is a deeply felt and weightily considered step on your part, not something thought up on the spur of the moment just to be in the swim or possibly catch up on some of your engaged friends.

More than likely she will sense it coming—girls are gifted in such psychic matters. But the boy must be prepared for possible confusion on her part, or indecision, if she really has not anticipated the moment.

She may ask for time to think it over, to examine her own heart. Or she may ask for a delay without turning down the proposal—time, perhaps, to finish her college studies; time to take a trip which was long planned, and which may help her to discover her own feelings more genuinely; or just a plea to continue the discussion at a later moment of her own choosing, when her own emotions may be as clear to her as those of the young man.

Whatever she may say of this nature, take it with tenderness and understanding. No doubt you are impatient for a direct answer—a yes or a no, without hedging—because the male animal is like that. But you've got to curb this feeling and be patient. You've proposed because you love her. You have a much better chance of proving it by a manly show of concern for her feelings than by trying to argue or bully her into a positive response when she isn't sure of herself. Besides being thoughtful, you're being smart by waiting: forcing her into an immediate decision may get you the wrong answer, even from a girl who'd like to say yes and still can't get herself to say it—yet.

The boy must understand that it is in the nature of girls to cling more closely to their families. There may be parental concerns which are really none of his business, at least at this time—the health of her mother or father, a difficult economic situation which may clear up soon, reservations on the parents' side concerning *him* (impossible? well, you know how parents are!)—or other personal considerations of her own, respecting age, hopes for a career, or the like, which she might not want to discuss with him without a little consideration of her own or perhaps advice from the outside. So, young man, be patient. And no less affectionate and loving. You have stated your case: stand by it.

Of course, if the unthinkable really comes to pass and she turns down the proposal, all that is left is a dignified retreat and acceptance of her decision in a sporting and gentlemanly manner.

Naturally, if a girl breaks out in guffaws when a fellow proposes to her, is too preoccupied with her make-up to hear what he is saying, or responds with some jocular phrase such as "Get lost!" this gives him an opportunity to see that he never had a chance anyway, and lessens the necessity for responding on such a lofty plane as we've been discussing. However, nothing she can say should elicit any bitter or critical reprisals from the rejected suitor. He is defeated but must retire in good order, if only for his own self-respect.

More than likely, a girl trying to turn down a proposal will do everything in her power to be considerate. If she takes refuge in the banal "But we'll always be friends, won't we?" there is little need to reply that the staggering outlays of cash for dinner, theater, and other amusements were not intended solely as gestures of comradeship, and will be forthwith either discontinued outright, or at least reduced drastically in amount. Let it be. Assure her that friends it is, forever, and that you realize her answer has been sincere. You are grateful for it. You admire her for it. You will never forget her. But you may not see her as often as in the past, because it would not be right. *Ave et vale.*

He buys the engagement ring

It is not absolutely essential that there be an engagement ring. But it is better when there is.

The boy will find that it is a highly persuasive gesture, while making his proposal, to produce the engagement ring from his pocket, and make gestures preparatory to putting it on the finger of his beloved.

His beloved will surely be hard-pressed at this point not to accept, and if she does, there won't be much doubt left in his mind about her really meaning it.

The ring doesn't have to be particularly expensive, either. The modern preference is for a diamond, and of course no good diamond could be called cheap. Its cost should be appropriate both to the importance of the occasion and to the boy's means, equally. This is a sentimental occasion, not one for display or investment, and many a small, perfect diamond has been treasured far more than an emerald cut.

The man who decides to purchase the engagement ring himself, in advance, should go to the best jeweler in his community and discuss his problem with him in complete frankness. The jeweler will advise him as to the most fashionable and desirable settings, and counsel him as to the value of the diamond he will be getting within his price range. It is important to deal with the most reputable store in this matter. There is a good chance of being taken in by some less responsible merchant who advertises huge stones at bargain rates. Another point to keep in mind is that the girl will probably be going to the store of purchase for a correct fitting to her finger, and of course she will appreciate his thoughtfulness in bringing her to a well-established store. Beware the "I can get it for you wholesale" friend at this time. It isn't worth all the possible grief that may lie beyond that famous, and sometimes infamous, phrase.

If you find that a diamond is beyond your means, there are other precious stones equally treasured—an emerald, ruby, sapphire, or pearl. Or perhaps you'd rather wait until you've proposed and then suggest that you shop for the ring together. And don't forget the many economical alternatives. Sometimes a gem that has been a family possession over generations may serve very happily as the engagement ring, adding to the sentiment. In that case the man should offer to have the stone reset in the modern manner, so that it may be more personally a part of the engagement. It is perfectly acceptable for him to use an heirloom from his own family in this way, or even to accept a stone from his fiancée's family.

Another very happy possibility is to adopt the girl's birthstone as the center of the engagement ring. In a setting of her own choosing, this has wonderfully romantic sentiment, and a very special meaning. All the birthstones are beautiful.

January		garnet
February		amethyst
March		aquamarine or bloodstone
April		diamond*
May		emerald
June		pearl or moonstone
July		ruby
August		onyx
September		sapphire
October		opal or tourmaline
November		topaz
December		turquoise

An engagement ring is worn for the first time on the day the engagement is announced. (The announcement itself is up to the family of the girl.) The slender circle of modern engagement rings does not accommodate the sentimental quotations once cherished by brides of another day. Instead, it will be marked with the first initials of the engaged pair, and the date scaled down to a mere notation, such as 2–10–64.

He confesses all to her family

The young man who has just been accepted by his girl no longer has to appear before her father and plead for her hand. He already has it. But it is still good form to present yourself to her father as a courtesy due him. After your girl has accepted you, ask her father promptly if you may see him for the purpose of discussing your future together with his daughter. Make no bones about what you're going to see him for.

Of course, he is apt to have had some inkling in advance of all this. And you are apt to know how he feels about it. But it is just as frequently the case that you may not live in the same community as

* Be sure of her birthday in advance on this one.

your girl, and perhaps your courtship has not taken you to her home very often. It is only fair, therefore, to announce to her father your intentions and plans. Don't take any drinks before the meeting—that is silly, and will only make you seem immature in his eyes. If he's the man you hope he is, he's apt to offer you one anyway, either during or after your conversation.

As simply and straightforwardly as possible, give him an outline of your future as you see it. Tell him what you make at the moment, and your ideas as to how this may be increased in the future. Tell him something of your hopes and standards in the problems of maintaining a home, developing your career, and educating your family. You have to assume that your income and general economic position may seem rather slight to him, unless you are exceptionally gifted or fortunate, or he is an utter failure himself—in any of which cases, you have little to fear from his opinion as to your income. In most instances a sensible father agrees with his daughter, gives you his blessing, and hopes for the best. If, in spite of your stated ability to support his daughter, he has any objections to the marriage, discuss them with him respectfully and frankly. He may think that it is not yet time for his daughter to embark on a career as housewife and mother, and that's natural enough for any father to think. The cards are all in your hand, so you merely remind him gently that the decision is ultimately in his daughter's hands. If he just doesn't like you, and says so, or flatly states that you obviously can't support his daughter even in the style to which she is unaccustomed (he could be right, you know, and is merely telling you obliquely that *he* doesn't propose to go on paying his daughter's bills or support the two of you), you should carefully avoid a head-on collision. Say that you respect his point of view very much and will certainly talk it over at length with his daughter. Then you tell her about this, and she'll probably find ways and means of bringing the old boy around. Whatever you do, *don't* get into an out-and-out debate, and *don't* set up a situation that throws the girl on your side and against her own father.

He may ask that you wait a little while before you actually get

--⊰{ 19 }⊱--

married. This is a naturally cautious suggestion for a parent to make. If this is the gist of his objections—and at the heart of it is only his conviction that an engagement of reasonable duration will be a good test of the genuineness of your affections—prepare yourself to go

along with it. A young man in love is excusably headstrong—but not so headstrong as to alienate his fiancée's father or belittle his wisdom or loving concern. Make a few concessions, and you'll be happier in the end: fathers have been known to be very generous where their daughters are concerned, in thought as well as deed, and you have everything to gain, for her sake. And, of course, she's going to be all the prouder if her father gets along with you and comes to the conclusion that you're worthy of his daughter. (He won't admit that much, in his heart, nine times out of ten, but you've won your battle for all time when he reaches for your hand and murmurs something about that libation.)

If by reason of divorce or other immutable circumstance your fiancée's father is not on the premises, it is still your obligation to present yourself in the same manner to the individual who functions as the head of the household, whether guardian, older brother, or whoever.

Your girl's mother will have been in on the secret long ago, and your only obligation here is personal, not social. All you must do here is convince her that the qualities that you adore in your fiancée are obviously inherited from her mother's side. The battle, sir, can be that easily won—particularly if you mean it.

He presents his family to hers

If you're following the grand old American custom of marrying the girl next door, you have no further social problems anent the families, who will be shortly discussing it all over the hedge, just as they may have previously discussed your birth and graduation from grammar school.

If, however, your own family is not known to her family, custom requires that your mother and father call upon your fiancée if they live within visiting distance. If they cannot call, they should write her as soon as they hear of the engagement from you. Your fiancée returns the visit, or answers the letter, as the case may be. Your parents may give a party for her in lieu of these calls, if desired. It needn't be large, but it is a pleasant occasion on which to introduce her to your other relatives and friends.

---◄{ 21 }►---

He spreads the good word

The man should write a few letters of a special nature before the engagement is formally announced in the newspapers by the girl's family. "Of a special nature" is an uptown phrase meaning that he's got to spill the beans to all former girl friends, letting them down easily, without the shock of learning it first from another source. If these have been "dates," it is assumed that there will be no more. And then, of course, there are other friends and relatives who should be informed merely to spread the good tidings.

In general, the ones you will be informing, of the latter category and not your old girls, will probably receive wedding invitations later on. So don't make the mistake of personally informing people who may stand the slightest chance of being overlooked later on.

He toes the mark

As soon as a young man's engagement is announced it is a good rule for him to buckle down to building up his health as well as his savings to a maximum, seeing his male companions only at the most salutary hours and under the mildest conditions, and bidding the other sex farewell en masse on a romantic basis. Tongues have been provided by nature with muscles of remarkable flexibility and staying power, and nothing delights the gossips more than to find you still squiring an old girl friend—or worse, a new one—about town while your little wife-to-be is bustling about with her mother readying her trousseau. You may do a number of things in perfectly good faith that others will misunderstand in perfectly bad faith, so you owe it to your fiancée to watch your step.

This, by the way, includes her. Don't appear to move in on her family too thoroughly, although of course you'll be in their company much more than formerly. Let us hope that her father does not request you to call him "Pop," but even if he does fall into such nonsense, the privilege does not automatically include rights to driving his automobile, answering the phone in his home, or using it indiscriminately for your own purposes, charging your drinks to him at the club, or in any other way suggesting to his community of friends that he didn't lose a daughter but gained a liability.

Your responsibilities extend even further than this in the area of good taste. Specifically, you've got to be a bit more formal with your fiancée until the wedding than you were when she was merely your "girl." Don't stay out too late with her. Don't go on any trips with her without adequate and visible chaperonage. Don't enter her apartment or home at such a time, or in such a manner, that any intimacy could be implied even by the most disinterested observer. If you and she have been accustomed to enjoying long and late dates together, occasionally of a hilarious nature, cut down on their length and hilarity. You can make up for it after you're married, when there'll be nothing to worry about except fallen arches and hangovers. But just now, it is your fiancée's reputation which might possibly suffer. You know what we're talking about very well. You can prove your love by protecting her in every way.

After all, that's the job you've taken on, isn't it?

--·⟩{ 23 }⟨·--

She says yes

In all right-thinking fiction and drama the heroine says yes, at least toward the end of the story, and all's right with the world.

No young lady needs any coaching in the art of charming acquiescence. The only suggestions that might be pertinent are in reference to her possible refusal.

If her answer is to be no, it should be done with tact and appreciation. After all, it is quite a compliment to be asked, and his sincerity deserves a like response. Under that heading, the young lady should never be unclear. It is an unkindness to leave him dangling and hopeful when there really is no hope for him at all. If you want to point out to him that there is still hope, based upon a plea for further consideration or simply a suggestion that the subject be put off for a while and definitely discussed at a later time, that is within the rules. If it is the truth that you don't want to get married just now and that is the reason for turning him down, tell him so, and it will help his self-esteem. But, of course, don't marry someone else within the month. It would indicate a slight deceitfulness in your personality.

If he presents you with a ring, *fait accompli,* it probably will not be difficult to adore it. If he does not have a ring but thinks that you should go shopping for one together, it is up to you to be extremely sensitive concerning the amount he has to lay out for it. It has been suggested that a young man should huddle in advance with his jeweler in order to establish a practical range of price: in that case, you are free to choose within the gems shown to you.

It is understandable that a young lady, faced with a showcase of diamonds, might match their sparkle with something similar in her eye, especially when that blue orb falls on something really spectacular in a flawless stone. A little self-discipline is indicated here. A young man should be full of love and bravery to embark upon marriage, but not necessarily money. That exquisite ring in the center of the showcase may be far more suitable as an anniversary gift later on, when your young man is a fast-moving executive, and perhaps it would look more appropriate on your finger then, too. So let us settle for something beautiful, within his means, charming, and in a setting which bespeaks your own personality.

She formally announces the engagement

The girl writes to her friends and relatives, giving them the happy news in advance of the engagement. She is particularly careful to be thoughtful in those letters which may come under the "Dear John" category, informing disappointed suitors of the event.

It is at this point, of course, that the family of the girl steps in firmly and faces with inutterable calm the really formidable financial burdens of a formal engagement and wedding. Fortunately, all those who have been through it and survived are free to say that it is one of the most enjoyable ways in the world to spend money, and fathers have been known to enjoy the festivities even more than anyone else on the scene.

The parents often announce the engagement at a luncheon, tea, or dinner. It may be an intimate affair for family and close friends, or a larger party with many guests. The point must be borne in mind that most of the guests will expect to attend the wedding as well, so the size of the engagement party may best be estimated according to the wedding plans. If there is a party, an announcement is sent to the press ahead of time, to be published the day following.

The engagement may be announced with equal propriety solely by a notice in the city or cities where the families of the girl and her fiancé live. Newspapers are interested in such news, of course, for their social columns, and will give it as much prominence as conflicting events of that day permit. If the young lady has been prominent socially in her community, a picture of her might accompany the announcement when it is sent to the newspaper. The announcement itself should be purely factual, and typewritten or legibly written by hand. Don't call up the newspaper office and expect them to take down the information over the phone. Here is a suggested letter for the occasion:

The Editor
Society News Department
The *Daily Beacon*
Bay City, New York

Dear Madame:

My husband and I are announcing the engagement of our daughter, Mary Ann Jerome, to Mr. James Martin Noble, of Quincy, Massachusetts, the son of Doctor and Mrs. Henry Jordan Noble of that city. He is the grandson of Mr. and Mrs. Samuel Clayton of Marlboro, Massachusetts, and the late Mr. and Mrs. Mathew Noble of Cleveland, Ohio. Mr. Noble was General Manager of Federated Stores, Inc., at the time of his death in 1950.

Mr. Noble is a graduate of (give name of high school or preparatory school), class of 1956, and graduated from Bryson University in 1960. He served (give his armed forces service record). He is presently with the Quincy Branch of Associated Motors.

My daughter graduated from Friends School, and from Cumberland University, class of 1962, where she majored in Markets and Merchandise, and is now with Sholto & Co., in New York City.

An April wedding is planned.

I hope that you will be able to use this notice in your issue of February 12th, as we are announcing the engagement at a small dinner on the 11th.

A recent photograph of my daughter is enclosed, which I trust you may also be able to use.

Sincerely yours,
Clara Boyd Jerome
(Mrs. Charles Major Jerome)

Identical letters should be sent to the newspapers in the cities where the family of the young man lives, as well as to newspapers where either family in the past has had long association.

She decides, en famille, on the kind of wedding

This is the very first decision that a bride-elect is called upon to make. She should do this with great care and consideration of the expense involved to her family. Most parents anticipate this occasion and are prepared to give their daughter pretty much what she wants in the way of a wedding. There are, after all, many ways in which to expand or contract the plans for a wedding, as we shall see later, and the basic cost should not be prohibitive.

The bride-elect will find in most cases that her fiancé would like to have as simple a wedding as possible and then to depart practically in secret—most young men are not social-minded in this respect. However, unless she is distinctly of the same thought, it must be pointed out that a wedding is an affair that gives pleasure to other members of two entire families and the whole circle of friends connected with both. It is not a display but a ceremony, and being a landmark in the family history, the popular decision is usually to do it in the best style permissible. Any bride who has been married at a formal wedding never forgets the memories and spiritual uplift of the affair, as well as the glamor of being the central figure in our civilization's most significant rite.

In making her decision, the bride decides whether the wedding shall be formal or informal, depending entirely upon the costume she elects. If she chooses full bridal array, gown and veil, the wedding is formal; if she wears a short wedding dress, or a going-away costume, the wedding is informal. Since the bride's gown undeniably sets the pattern for every facet of the wedding and reception, and especially for what is worn by the members of the bridal party as well as by the guests, if her costume is to be formal, the wedding, to be consistent, carries the obligation of formal dress.

She sets up a timetable

June is still by far the preferred month for weddings. September, with October a popular contender, is tied for second place. But in these times every month seems to be a bridal month, and owing to the lure of honeymoons in the South or snowy North, winter weddings are much more frequent than they were a few decades back. The focal point in most cases is the ability of the young man to take a vacation from his job. This favors June, but since winter vacations are becoming almost equally fashionable, there seems to be plenty of choice.

There is no favorite day of the week. Fridays and the thirteenth of the month are avoided by people who have no superstitions but still don't want to stir up sleeping pixies. Saturdays were formerly scorned by the *haut monde,* but the practical idea of adding the weekend to the length of the honeymoon is well worth considering.

High noon or twelve thirty is the fashionable hour for a morning wedding; four o'clock for an afternoon wedding. If the ceremony takes place as late as five o'clock and the reception lasts until six or later, it is still classed as an afternoon wedding.

The approved hour for a formal evening wedding is eight thirty.

This is also the time of day chosen in those portions of the South or West where the heat of earlier daylight hours must be taken into consideration.

Catholic weddings are often scheduled as early as eight o'clock in the morning, and many a Catholic Nuptial Mass is celebrated in the

afternoon. (This will be developed later on, as will be the Jewish wedding.)

The number of things to be done, remembered, and double-checked on a wedding schedule are so monumental that one is tempted to borrow a term from a far less agreeable activity, war, and conclude that the *logistics* of it all require a certain amount of staff or executive ability.

We will cover a great many "things to do," but it's almost as important to set aside adequate time to do them as it is to get them in the works.

The bride should allow herself a twelve-week period to get her preparations under way, and after that she should proceed steadily and methodically, according to a set schedule. She probably could do it all in six or eight weeks, if she is willing to put in an overtime effort. But, human nature being what it is, she must expect delays in deliveries, and slips of a minor or major nature all along the line, and it's a good idea to spare herself the nervous pressures arising from this kind of disappointment. So, let's line up these plans on a do-or-sigh timetable:

A. *12 to 10 weeks prior to the wedding:*
   1. Decide on formal or informal wedding.
   2. Decide where: church, hotel, club or at home.
   3. Set date and hour, and settle arrangements with minister.
   4. Make church, hotel, or club reservations if wedding not at home.
   5. Engage caterer if reception is to be at home.
   6. Establish budget figure and set down tentative items of expense.
   7. Interview florist, musical director, decorators, and stationer for wedding invitations and announcements.

B. *10 to 8 weeks prior to wedding:*
   1. Begin lists of guests of family and your own personal friends.
   2. Obtain list of guests of fiancé's family and his personal friends.
   3. Check both lists to avoid duplications.
   4. Choose bridal party.
   5. Check estimates received against budget figures and determine money available for trousseau.
   6. Decide on patterns for silver, china, glassware, and linens, and list them with shops.
   7. Start shopping for wedding costume and personal trousseau.

C. *8 to 6 weeks prior to wedding:*
   1. Make final check-up on guest list.
   2. Begin shopping for lingerie.
   3. Order invitations.
   4. Order wedding costume, and dresses for attendants.
   5. Approve estimates of florist, decorator, and music, and make contracts for them.

D. *6 to 4 weeks prior to wedding:*
1. Address and stamp invitations.
2. Check up on your current wardrobe for trousseau holdovers.
3. Finish all shopping.

E. *4 weeks to 1 week prior to wedding:*
1. Mail all invitations.
2. Have final fitting of wedding gown, and arrange for photographs.
3. Contract for movies or candids for your wedding and for tape recording of wedding and reception to be a permanent part of your family memorabilia.
4. Record and acknowledge wedding gifts as they arrive.
5. Order wedding cake and decide on menu for wedding breakfast or reception.
6. Select and buy gifts for bridal party, and plan luncheon for their presentation.
7. Arrange living quarters for out-of-town guests at home, club, or hotel.
8. Check delivery of all trousseau purchases.

F. *Last week prior to wedding:*
1. Present gifts to bridesmaids at dinner or luncheon.
2. Display gifts at tea.
3. Groom's bachelor dinner. This is his obligation unless given for him by best man and ushers.
4. Dinner for all members of the wedding party. Wedding rehearsal may be before or after it.
5. WEDDING DAY

All these plans will be discussed in greater detail elsewhere in this book, which is arranged chronologically. But at this time, it becomes the bride to survey her kingdom, standing like Cortez on a peak, and with wild surmise to recognize the multiplicity of all that must be done before saying "I do."

She draws up a budget

The time to draw up a budget is *now*—when you are sure that you're going to be a bride but haven't made any commitments as yet on expenditures. If you don't look at them in advance, when the choice is a simple matter of yes or no, the time may come when these expenses arrive not in the form of estimates but bills.

The expenses belong by tradition to the bride's family. And her father, by tradition, is the harassed and set-upon individual who pays bills beyond his means and certainly beyond his dreams. Although the caricature of the furrow-browed father is frequently overdone, the bride should be careful that her demands and wishes are in some kind of sensible proportion to her father's means. She is nominally in charge of her wedding, but the head of her household has the power of the veto, invested in his checkbook. The first step is to establish a working understanding between father and daughter that includes frankness but also a capacity for concession on both sides.

The groom gets off lightly. He buys the license and rings, bouquets and corsages, boutonnieres for his ushers and a few personal gifts for them, a gift for his bride, he sets aside a gift for the officiating minister, and that's it.

The bride's father does not have any obligation to pay for the hotel accommodations for any of the guests, although he will undoubtedly make the necessary reservations for them in order to ease the perplexities of the situation. He may decide to put up the groom or members of the groom's family, or special guests of the bride or her family, at his own club. In that case it would probably prove an embarrassment in a number of ways if he did not foot the bill. But the choice is entirely up to him.

The bride's attendants and the groom's ushers pay for their own clothes and accessories, but that's about the only break the father of the bride gets. All the rest goes on his tab.

Now, of course, there is a tremendous range of costs, depending upon geographical factors, the social importance of the bride's family, the degree of formality of the wedding, etc. The best way to approach the matter is to look a fairly formal wedding squarely in the eye and then try to see where the variants may throw a favorable balance toward the economy side. After all, a bride may buy a formal gown for thousands of dollars, or she may spend less than a hundred for it. However, there are certain inescapable facts of life to be faced in this matter. A pretty gown may cost only $125; fashionable stores advertise wedding gowns in fashionable magazines for about $225, with veil and headdress extra, and the ensemble is usually stunning; after that, the bride may soar to any heights she and her father can weather as to the altitude of the figure on the price tag.

So let us first look at the items that must be paid for, and then set some sort of a calculating range of probable prices for them.

This covers "the works."

Let us assume that this is to be a wedding in a church at four o'clock, with a dozen attendants to the bride, and a country club reception afterward (or perhaps in a midtown club or hotel) with dancing and hot buffet for about two hundred guests. The setting can be in a suburb of a large city, or perhaps in a city of some 250,000 inhabitants. The range of expenses is upward of medium· in a large city with metropolitan tastes, most of the expenses would be upped another twenty-five per cent. And, of course, there are plenty of economies possible to bring the total figure down. But these are the stark facts of a fashionable wedding. The items marked with an asterisk are essential; the others are optional.

FOR THE WEDDING CEREMONY

Item	Price Range	
* Gown	$150 to	$300
* Veil or headdress	35	100
* Personal accessories	25	75
* Gifts to bridesmaids	24	120
* Bouquets for bridesmaids	96	154
* Decorative flowers	100	150
* Invitations	25	75
* Organist	10	50
Cars for bridal party	75	100
Canopy for church entrance	100	150

--⊰ FOR THE WEDDING CEREMONY ⊱--

Item	Price Range	
Sexton	$ 25 to	$ 50
Pew ribbons	20	35
Candles	25	35
Aisle runner	25	60
Formal photograph	50	150
Tip to traffic officer	10	25
Total	$795 to $1,629	

--⊰ FOR THE RECEPTION ⊱--

Item	Price Range	
* Champagne or punch (18 cases)	$ 700 to	$1,000
* Cake	50	100
* Decorative flowers	100	250
Additional beverages	500	1,000
Rent for room, service, tips, etc.	175	300
Photographer (candids)	75	200
Souvenirs	100	200
Menu per person ($7.50 to $15.00, for 200 guests)	1,500	3,000
Music for listening (5 pieces)	150	200
Music for dancing	500	1,000
Miscellaneous	250	275
Total	$4,100 to	$7,525
GRAND TOTAL	$4,895 to	$9,154

It is clear, then, that Dad needs an extra five to ten thousand if he really wants to stage a wedding that is "fashionable." It could come to much more, of course. More guests, the probability of an informal party the night before for family and close friends, as well as a luncheon before the ceremony, might send the tab soaring beyond. And of course there are certain uncontrollable items, particularly that of "additional beverages." Several hundred people in a festive mood can run up quite a bill at an open bar.

Later on in this guidebook each of these items will be taken up separately and in detail: its worth questioned and evaluated, its financial probabilities examined carefully. But for the moment this is the long view that the bride-elect and her father must take before deciding on the character of the wedding.

Now, of course, lots of young people get married at charming and memorable weddings that cost nowhere in the neighborhood of that we have been discussing. And a few cost quite a bit more. But let's adjust our budget to something more modest. Here is a projection on a home ceremony and a reception for thirty guests:

Item	Price Range	
Gown, headdress	$130 to	$200
Accessories	25	50
Maid of honor's gift	10	25
Maid of honor's bouquet	10	25
Flowers for mantel and tables	15	30
Invitations	5	15
Champagne	55	75
Cake	15	40
Refreshments (ice cream, nuts, mints)	20	40
Service for occasion	10	25
Photographer (candids)	50	150
Total	$345 to	$675

This probably will leave Dad breathing a little easier. A wedding, thus, can be a tremendous social event or a home gathering, with the prices in accord. For now, then, the bride has surveyed her bridal territory and taken in its topographical features. She is in a position to tell with some certainty how high she wishes to climb.

She is never too busy to love

One of the inevitabilities of every wedding is the focus of attention on the bride. It is Her Day. She is the cynosure. She is the fairy princess.

The groom, on the other hand, is a faintly comical creation of the occasion.

Having reached his peak of recognition long in advance of the wedding—in fact, at the moment of proposal—he then slides back into a limbo of inattention from which he barely emerges even at the moment of placing the wedding ring on his bride's finger.

No one cares much what he proposes to wear, since he is fettered to ironbound rules dictated by convention. The bride is free as a bird to enjoy the beauteous variations possible on the theme of her wedding dress, but the groom must look like every other groom, and his perfection in his part depends upon a complete denial of any individuality.

He finds himself immediately caught up in a welter of plans—concerning dresses, flowers, and other rituals of the occasion—on which his opinion may infrequently be asked only to be disregarded. The suspicion grows in the community in which his wife has resided (possibly all her life) that she has thrown herself away on a cross between a barbarian and a wastrel and that his fiancée would have done better, after all, to have accepted that Jones boy who had been mooning around her for so many years. Dull type, but reliable.

The groom, imprisoned by the monastic requirements of his affianced state, finds his only social delights in anticipating a wing-ding called the bachelor dinner, which will cost him a pretty penny, only to be derided and pelted with satyrical humor by a bunch of cronies he could have seen any time over a couple of beers.

Even his entrance into the wedding picture is a low-key performance. While his bride drives in regal state to the church, and sweeps up the aisle in the grand pageant of the traditional wedding, the groom and his best man cower like cravens in the wings. Stashed away in some corner of the vestry, they see no one but themselves for the long minutes awaiting the bride's arrival at the altar, and then file into the church sheepishly before turning their backs on the wedding guests.

This long penance of the groom, from engagement to marriage, has its compensations afterward, in full, as the appendage of "Mr." reaches its full estate, perhaps for the first time in his life. It is not anything to make him bury his head in his pillow at night and to cause him to break out into loud, anguished sobs, but he can't help feeling a little out of it in the whirlwind of orchids, lace, and froufrou. His little bride-to-be, keyed up by the sustained requirements of the

run to the altar, may also find that she's often too busy even to see her Romeo and, if she does, becomes bemused by her problems and absent-mindedly confuses his image with visions of hems, gores, snaps, puffs, and wisps of tulle. It's a trying time for the man.

Brides must remember this. It isn't a matter of his feelings being hurt—they won't be. But his affections may undergo a bit of a puzzle-ment. He won't have any *doubts* about you. But he'll begin to question his previously uninterrupted lines of communication. That is why it is important for you to be both sensitive and sensible, and to take extra precautions at the height of your busiest preparations. Keep him informed as to the fact that he is the leading person in your life, if not in the wedding pageant. That certainly shouldn't be too hard for you to do.

They buy the wedding ring

We took the romantic viewpoint in advising the groom to purchase his engagement ring in advance because it struck us that if you're not going to be romantic over getting engaged, then there's no hope for you at all in that direction.

However, it is not considered hopelessly businesslike at such a time to purchase the ring together. This takes into consideration the fact that the girl has to wear the ring, and should be pleased with it in its entirety, loving it as a beautiful treasure as well as a symbol of her sweetheart's affection. Under this reasoning, therefore, the young couple may journey to the jeweler together for the dual purpose of buying the engagement ring and the wedding ring on the same trip.

The young lady is supposed to have a feeling of mercy at such times, and make such choices that do not compel her groom-to-be to rob a bank in order to meet his obligations. A sensible way to release her from such a troubling dilemma is for the young man to phone ahead to the jeweler with a suggestion as to the price ranges he can afford for the rings, and thus have the girl be presented only with choices among the realistic price levels of his income. Another way might be for the young man to precede her on a visit to the jeweler, which would leave him free to discuss prices and what they will mean in terms of rings, and this would leave him free to make adjustments in his own calculations without the obvious embarrassment of having to do this in the presence of the girl.

From there on out, it is a matter of which is her choice and what they may decide together as the best wedding ring design. The custom of a double-ring ceremony has recently grown in popularity. (When we were married, it was considered quite old-fashioned, but that was in the first year of World War II. A little later a man going into Service thought of times when a wedding ring on his finger might be his only link to home, and so the double-ring ceremony quickly became first choice.) The rings are usually similar in design, although there is no rule specifying that they should be. If the groom is to wear a ring, the bride pays for it.

(A small anecdote about double-ring ceremonies comes to mind. As best man, Fred B. was once required to carry both rings for a double-ring ceremony, and at the given moment when the best man is expected to reach into his pocket and produce what is necessary with absolute surety and grace, he came up with only one ring—the man's! After much looking around in pockets, and much head shaking and shuffling of feet by the assembled guests, it was discovered that the ring for the bride, who had a tiny hand, had fitted so exactly into the groom's that they had become one—a throwback to the ancient geminal symbolism in a modern marriage ceremony, and a happy one, even though it held it up for quite a few painful minutes and promised to disrupt the plans for a double-ring wedding. The rings were duly separated, placed on their respective hands, and the best man breathed easier.)

Neither bride nor groom *ever* wears the wedding ring until it has been placed on the hand during the marriage ceremony. An engagement ring may be worn in advance of the announcement of the engagement only if the bride is sure of her parents' consent in advance.

They may cancel the engagement, if they must

Human nature being what it is, perfection is not always just around the corner, and sometimes it is just the wise and sensible thing to realize that a mistake has been made and an engagement should be broken. If there is any doubt about the engagement on the part of either the man or the girl, it should be brought out into the open and discussed seriously and carefully. It is far better to endure the pain and embarrassment of calling off an engagement than to go ahead "for the sake of appearances" and proceed into a marriage that can only result in unhappiness. But at the same time, breaking an engagement which has been entered into in all good heart is also a serious matter and one that involves more than just a few words of discussion.

Some psychiatrists and all grandparents are familiar with the doubts that assail both man and woman after an engagement is announced. Perhaps it does not always happen, but it is not an unusual thing for both of them to have a case of the jitters at that point. On his side, he

is subject to plenty of jokes and raillery from his well-meaning friends on the loss of his freedom, the financial strains of paying for two on the same old salary, and the good things of life he will be forgoing for other good things he has elected. It is, alas, true that two cannot live as cheaply as one: two can only live as cheaply as three, in terms of what a bachelor assumes is a normal living expenditure for a single person, aside from amusement, which takes up most of his funds. He begins to have his secret fears. This turns into a far more critical attitude toward his fiancée than he was wont to sport during the furious hours, days, and months of the chase, when she seemed superior to all mortals in all ways. He looks at her now, and he sees just a girl—beloved and dear, but mortal. He is shaken. He wonders if mind and heart are at odds within him.

Meanwhile, she looks at him, and she is not merely shaken but absolutely rent. *This* coarse clay, this bumpkin, this lout, can he be the Galahad who won her heart? Are these ill-chosen jests his wit? This indecision the mark of a leader? This incompetence a sign of future accomplishment? Her little heart contracts. She sees loving parents with new eyes, as paragons of understanding and affection.

There may be sharp words. There may be spats. There may be fights. After all, they are playing the married role—almost—but without its most priceless rewards. It is a time of some questioning, some uncertainty, and, possibly, doubt.

So, anticipate these feelings. They may possibly not even make themselves known. They may be mild. They may be extreme. In any case, know in advance, you two, that you are not the first to be so assailed. Take it slow if you have your doubts. Talk it over with people who care most for you, and with people who might have had some experience under similar circumstances.

Then, and only then, break the engagement if you must.

When we were researching this book, we found that in one year there were only three of the heartbreaking announcements in the *New York Times,* but they were there. Usually because a previous public announcement had been made. Friends, of course, can be told privately. But a short newspaper announcement may be necessary if the principals have been close to a wide social scene and a large number of people had been reached by the previous announcement. The form of the announcement of the broken engagement is invariable:: "The engagement of Miss ⸺ ⸺ and Mr. ⸺ ⸺ has been terminated (or broken) by mutual consent."

At this sad point all engagement presents must be returned with a short thank-you note and, if desired, a repetition of the termination announcement. Regardless of how the engagement came to be broken, the ring goes back to the now groom-not-to-be, unless the stone came from the bride's family. In that case, even if the groom had the ring put into a new setting it still remains with the bride. *Eheu.*

They visit their clergyman early

If the young couple is to be married by a clergyman, they should visit him as soon as possible after the engagement announcement.

He is quite an important gentleman in the wedding.

It is up to him to decide as to whether he will marry you or not. The chances are that he will be the clergyman who has been known to the bride and her family for many years, in which case she makes the appointment to see him. The groom makes the appointment if the clergyman is "his" or if the gentleman has not been previously known to either of them.

This is a serious moment, to all parties. The couple should dress as carefully for it as if attending church, and should be prompt to the second.

He is a man of the Faith and he is going to act like one. If one or both of the couple are known to him, he will probably not be too searching in his questions. But he will under any circumstances be inclined to discuss the spiritual aspects of your decision, and will want to know certain aspects of your background—baptism, confirmation, and recent church attendance and affiliation. If the couple are not of the same denomination or faith, he may decide that religious instruction for one or both will be in order so that the ceremony will be more meaningful.

Once he is satisfied that the wedding has been planned with the proper spiritual background, the clergyman will then be the key figure in deciding as to the day and the time of the ceremony. The couple may, of course, suggest the day they prefer, but the clergyman's word on this is law. He has his entire church schedule to consider, and there are other religious proprieties in his mind as to the Church calendar and its relation to the wedding.

Every detail must be discussed with him after his consent has been obtained. At this or a later interview he must be apprised of the details of the plans as the family would like them, i.e., the size of the wedding party, the number of guests expected, what music is desired, the proposed decoration of the church, the costuming of the wedding party, the use of candles and other paraphernalia. If there is going to be a rehearsal, he should decide upon the time for this.

The occasion might arise in which an out-of-town clergyman, a special friend of either the bride or groom, might be asked to officiate. In this case, the plan is fully discussed with the clergyman whose church is to be used, his permission asked, and his suggestions requested as to the proper procedures. He may elect to participate in the ceremony as well. In any case, he receives a fee as well as the visiting clergyman. The visiting clergyman's travel expenses and hotel accommodations will be borne by the one who has invited him—the groom, or the bride's family.

Let me not to the marriage of true minds
Admit impediments. Love is not love
Which alters when it alteration finds,
Or bends with the remover to remove.
O no! It is an ever-fixed mark
That looks on tempests and is never shaken.
It is the star to every wandering bark,
Whose worth's unknown, although his height be taken.
Love's not Time's fool, though rosy lips and cheeks
Within his bending sickle's compass come.
Love alters not with his brief hours and weeks,
But bears it out even to the edge of doom.
  If this be error and upon me proved,
  I never writ, nor no man ever loved.

WILLIAM SHAKESPEARE

Chapter Three

✿

Here Comes the Bride

Now is the time that should be of great rejoicing, and in fact it is. But there also creeps into the daily lives of all of the members of the wedding, particularly the bride's family, and even the lucky girl herself, a series of such decisions to make and such to-and-fro scurryings—all of them over and above requirements of usual living—that frequently a real pressure situation can arise.

Dad is actually the top man of the entire event, although no one is going to give him any credit for being so, naturally. There was a recent case in the newspapers of the father of three daughters who had tired of the long campaign to put them through school, glamorize and clothe them, supply suitable transportation in the form of convertibles, etc. Contemplating the possibilities suggested by the thought of three splendiferous weddings, he quailed and summoned his three daughters into his presence. Then he made them a proposition. It was, simply, an offer to each of them of five hundred dollars in cash, and an eloping ladder.

This evasive action aside, Dad is confronted during the prenuptial period with soul-taxing expenses, and it is unlikely that even the most wealthy tycoon expects his family to confuse him with the custodian of Fort Knox. The way for the family to work it out is to set up one of the budgets outlined in the previous chapter and, with Dad's okay on whatever figure is decided upon, to get on with it. There's not much sense in discussing too many of the details with him. The poor man is in shock: he might even forget the decisions made previously on the total outlay, and launch a guerrilla campaign to reduce the cost of every item as it comes up. That won't do at all. The best plan is to go smilingly about the business at hand, and give him glowing reports on the general progress being made. No complaints, please: there were not any from him at the outset. On the other hand, if there are really certain instances where it looks as though the budget isn't quite going to make it, or perhaps a decision to spend a little more now might mean a great deal more value in the end, then Dad should be brought into the conference and let in on the secret of how much more it's going to cost him.

Mother, of course, no matter how shy and retiring she may be by nature, must suddenly become the skipper on the bridge and direct the entire voyage. And we're not about to give that lady any advice at all, except to extend our most affectionate good wishes. By this time in her life, she is probably ready for just about anything, and having survived the normal vicissitudes of a full family life—with probably a war or two, plus some natural disasters thrown in—she is unlikely to quail before the mere logistics of a marriage.

This brings us to the principals in the wedding. It is even more taxing for them, actually. Things will be done for them, it is true, but there are certain personal decisions to be made at this time which will have an important bearing on the happiness of everyone concerned, including themselves.

And so we might well pause and consider some of the things that should be buzzing through the mind of the groom.

To begin with, he must accustom himself to the curious manner in which wedding engagements are received by our often unpredictable society. There is usually a universal outpouring of joy on behalf of the bride-to-be. Her parents show him a beaming side that he had never before observed in quite this degree. His darling's girl friends go off into transports of delight. Her former boy friends become avuncular and somewhat possessive.

This has an odd effect on our hero. It strikes him that her parents seem more pleased at the thought of her being married than they should be. Was she as popular as he had supposed? What about those offers of marriage with which she had been deluged—according to rumor and implication delicately thrust at him—up to the very hour of *his* proposal? Could it possibly be that the family was, to put it indelicately, happy to catch a sucker who was willing to take the girl off their hands for life? His bride's girl friends seem overjoyed on her behalf, it is true, but they crowd around her in a manner that unmistakably calls to his mind the rooters congratulating the winning pitcher after a World Series ball game, or a quarterback who has just pulled out a close one with a last-second touchdown pass. Her former boy friends treat him with a strange mixture of sorrow and mystery, as if to say; "Boy, we'd like to tell you some of the things we know about her and her past, but that wouldn't quite be cricket, you know. Anyway, you'll find out in the long run—after it's too late."

Everyone he meets, however, assures him that he's the luckiest man in the world to have caught such a girl. He gets the impression, though, that the true meaning behind these greetings is not so much that he has got himself a veritable angel but that there is some slight wonderment abroad over how such an obviously inferior clown could have hoodwinked a perfectly nice girl into accepting him.

Even the remarks of his own friends seem to take on this hooded quality.

"Well, we'll certainly miss you, old boy."

"Have you told *Mary* yet?"

"Better buy yourself a few good suits right away, buster. Later on you won't have the dough."

Well, the best advice is to grin and bear it. During this time nobody's really interested in the groom. The bride's the thing, and now that you've popped the question and given her the ring, you're on the sidelines until they play the Processional "Wedding March" and even that will find you skulking in a closet somewhere in the vestry. Your job now is to settle down and get a grip on yourself. Make allowances for everyone: her family, her girl friends, and even those smirking boy friends of hers. You are approaching one of the true tests of man's estate, so you must meet it like a man.

You must anticipate, too, a change in the one-and-only girl. You never thought it could happen. But it will. At least, it will seem to be happening. It will now strike you that a change is coming over her that may make it seem that she was keeping one side of her under wraps all the while before. Where is that girl who liked to walk in the rain? Where now have fled the windblown hair and the un-adorned, careless face, with its classic beauty never needing make-up? Where is your intellectual companion of yore who talked hour after hour of Tolstoy and Beethoven's quartets and Poulenc and Miles Davis and the glories of Bach's chorales?

No more long silences that said so much. No more phone calls just to say "I love you." No more letters, written ten minutes after you left her, and received an hour before you see her on the following day. Alas, she has been replaced by a strange creature who seems to talk only of dresses and veils and drapes and shoes and flowers and invita-tions, and who has developed strange obsessions about your best friends and your family, mainly revolving about the thought that although they're a bunch of "dears" they stand their best chances of remaining that way by keeping at a distance. It looks to your aston-ished eyes as though you have become affianced to one of the most worldly and grasping females in the world, who is going to devote the rest of her life to acquiring clothes and helping tradesmen become millionaires.

True, at this moment it is not costing you a single cent. But there are portents abroad which seem to bode ill for the future.

The advice of this moment is: relax. She has been waiting for this time for the last half of her young life, and she has no more to say about what goes on—really—than a leaf has as it is borne along on a turbulent stream. And, to tell the truth, she likes it, too, being a true female. And why not? Let her enjoy her moment at the center of the stage. Let her be frivolous for now. Let her be foolish over foolish furbelows. Let her indulge in woman talk with her mother until you feel like going out of the house for a walk. In fact, do just that. They'll probably be more pleased than you are and, what's more, will give you an errand to run while you're about it.

Because the fact is, young sir, that to all intents and purposes you are already married in everyone's eyes except your own. And the truth of it is that you are now experiencing an excursion into a woman's world you have so blithely passed by before, glimpsed only as you sailed past your mother's room with a merry wave and a shouted word. It isn't going to hurt you. And as a matter of fact it is an excellent time in your life to come to certain excellent philosophical conclusions. They will be forced upon you sooner or later, and you'll be far better off if you take them up on your own terms.

I have never forgotten the truly great words of a truly great man, my father-in-law, spoken many years ago when I was in this same premarital dither. He and I were waiting outside Fran's home for her and her mother to finish their dressing and emerge so that we could take them out into the country for dinner. We were already late for others awaiting us there. My father-in-law, unperturbed himself, noticed my impatience. He spoke very quietly.

"You're going to spend thousands of hours of your life waiting for my daughter," he said. "That's just the way she is. So I'd suggest that you buy yourself Dr. Eliot's Five-Foot Shelf of Books, and whenever you find yourself waiting for Frances, you can pick up one of the books and just read until she comes along. Then later on in life, when you are being acclaimed for your wisdom and erudition, you can smile and say: 'I owe it all to my wife.'" Get the point? I did.

You may even think that your beloved has forgotten you now that she's got you. Don't fret about this. Of course she has, a little, because things aren't literally exactly the way they were before, and she's being distracted by a million things. Just bide your time. You'll have her to yourself all in due time. Just now your role is to be understanding and patient. If you're not, you'll be letting her down, and causing her to have some of these same disquieting thoughts concerning *you*.

So, see this one coming in advance. Brace yourself, and win through it with a minimum of concern, either in your own thoughts or aloud. It's all part of the show that's going on, and you're just one of the supporting cast of the Leading Lady.

He looks to the license

The man should take the responsibility for this all-important piece of paper. It has a way of seeming so innocent; yet at the same time, unless the details are all anticipated and worked out in advance with plenty of time to spare, the license could throw the whole wedding plan out of kilter.

It must be understood that the laws as to the age of consent, the taking of a blood test, and the amount of time before the license is issued, vary from state to state. The best plan is for the groom to look into the situation promptly, as soon as the engagement has been announced and the marriage date set, and then to fit in the time requirements into their overall schedule. The worst thing, of course, is to expect that this is a small matter which can be shoehorned in some time or another, when nothing else is taking place. That time will never come. Both parties must set a time and date for taking their blood tests and making the license application together.

See next page for a listing of state requirements. These are subject to change, of course, so it is best to check into them for each special case. Nonresidents in particular should double-check the requirements of an out-of-state marriage, and get the time factors down beyond doubt far in advance.

He submits a guest list to her family

This is not much of a problem for the groom. His own parents are part of the bridal party. He will want other close relatives to be present or to receive invitations even if they are not able or inclined to attend.

Beyond that, he selects those from among his friends whom he would like to honor at this time, and probably a few of his closest business associates.

The situation calls for some tact and careful thought on his part. It is not a matter of matching the bride's list with an equivalent one of his own. The marriage is to be held in her home or church, as a rule, and if he is from another part of the country, it is clear that the majority of the wedding guests will be from her community and these will be swelled by the relatives of the bride and the no-doubt considerable number of guests invited by the parents of the bride, friends who have accumulated over the course of many years. The groom must attend to his immediate family with his list, and then be entirely practical with the remainder. He will not invite guests at his future father-in-law's expense merely to impress them or to show off. Nor will he invite chums or acquaintances who have antisocial ideas or habits that will inevitably result in some kind of unhappy scene. The burden of

State	With Consent		Without Consent		Blood Test	Wait for License	Wait after License	License Fee, etc.
	Men	Women	Men	Women				
Alabama**	17	14	21	18	Required	None	None	$2.00
Alaska	18	16	21	18	Required	3 days	None	2.50
Arizona	18	16	21	18	Required	(i)	None	2.00
Arkansas	18	16	21	18	Required	3 days	None	3.00
California	18	16	21	18	Required	None	None	2.00
Colorado	16	16	21	18	Required	None	None	3.00
Connecticut	16	16	21	21	Required	4 days	None	2.00
Delaware	18	16	21	18	Required	None	(a)	3.00
District of Columbia	18	16	21	18	None	3 days	None	(b)
Florida	18	16	21	21	Required	3 days	None	3.00
Georgia	17	14	**	18	Required	None**	None	5.00
Hawaii	18	16	20	20	Required	4 days	None	5.00
Idaho	15	15	18	18	Required	None	None	3.00
Illinois*	18	16	21	18	Required	(i)	None	(c)
Indiana	18	16	21	18	Required	3 days	None	5.00
Iowa	18	16	21	18	Required	3 days	None	3.00
Kansas	18	16	21	18	Required	3 days	None	(d)
Kentucky	18	16	21	21	Required	3 days	None	6.00
Louisiana*	18	16	21	21	Required	None	72 hours	2.00
Maine	16	16	21	18	Required	5 days	None	2.00
Maryland	18	16	21	18	None	48 hours	None	(e)
Massachusetts	18	16	21	18	Required	3 days	None	*2.00
Michigan	18	16	18	18	Required	3 days	None	2.00
Minnesota	18	16	21	18	None	5 days	None	5.00
Mississippi**	17	15	21	18	Required	3 days	None	3.00
Missouri	15	15	21	18	Required	3 days	None	2.55
Montana	18	16	21	18	Required	5 days	None	2.25
Nebraska	18	16	21	21	Required	None	None	2.00
Nevada	18	16	21	18	None	None	None	5.00
New Hampshire*	h 14	h 13	20	18	Required	5 days	None	3.00
New Jersey*	18	16	21	18	Required	72 hours	None	3.00
New Mexico	18	16	21	18	Required	None	None	5.00
New York	16	14	21	18	Required	None	24 hrs. (j)	4.00
North Carolina*	16	16	18	18	Required	None	None	5.00
North Dakota*	18	15	21	18	Required	None	None	1.00
Ohio*	18	16	21	21	Required	5 days	None	2.15
Oklahoma**	18	15	21	18	Required	None	None	5.00
Oregon	18	15	21	18	Required	3 days	None	3.00
Pennsylvania	16	16	21	21	Required	3 days	None	3.00
Rhode Island**	18	16	21	21	Required	None*	None*	2.00
South Carolina	16	14	18	18	None	24 hrs. (i)	None	4.00
South Dakota	18	16	21	21	Required	None	None	2.50
Tennessee**	16	16	18	21	Required	3 days	None	2.00
Texas	16	14	21	18	Required	None	None	3.00
Utah	16	14	21	18	Required	None	None	2.50
Vermont*	18	16	21	18	Required	None	5 days	3.00
Virginia	18	16	21	21	Required	None	None	4.00
Washington	15	15	21	18	(g)	3 days	None	5.00
West Virginia	18	16	21	21	Required	3 days	None	2.00
Wisconsin	18	16	21	18	Required	5 days	None	1.50
Wyoming	18	16	21	21	Required	None	None	2.00
Canal Zone	17	14	21	18	None	None	None	2.00
Guam	18	16	21	18	None	None	None	2.50
Puerto Rico	18	16	21	21	(f)	None	None	None
Virgin Islands	16	14	21	18	None	8 days	None	40¢

* Special laws applicable to nonresidents.
** Special laws applicable to those under 21 years; Alabama—bond required if male is under 21 female under 18.
(a) 24 hours if one or both parties resident of state; 96 hours if both parties are nonresidents.
(b) 50¢ to file; $2.00 when license is issued. (c) Cook County, $5.00; balance of state, $3.00.
(d) $2.50 for license, plus $1.00 registration fee. (e) $3 to $6 depending upon county. (f) None, but a medical certificate is required. (g) None, but male must file affidavit. (h) Parental consent plus Court's consent required. (i) Wait for license from time blood test is taken; Arizona, 48 hours; Illinois, 1 day. (j) New York, marriage may not be solemnized within 3 days from date of blood test.

that distressing kind of thing is on him and not on them, and he had better think about that aspect of it in advance. Friends with excessive ideas as to their privileges in drinking, girl hunting, and other forms of hospitality, including long-distance phone calls, the abuse of servants or other employees—and he'll know all about this in advance if he's really known them—are types to whom it is better to tell the happy news after it's all over, permitting them to celebrate in their own special way. It is not the role of the groom to demonstrate to his father-in-law that good fellows from the poolroom should be democratically welcomed in the church or the receiving room, unless they are willing to take their cues from their host. He has taken no oath to put up with boors, and he should not be compelled to.

He selects his best man and his ushers

The selection here is never very difficult. The groom selects his best man, as the term implies—it may be his father, his brother, senior brother if he has more than one, or his best friend. Usually, his best man will be approximately his own age. This is a serious moment, and the selection of a best man will bind him to the groom virtually for life in this bond of indicated affection.

The ushers will be carefully chosen as well, and will usually be relatives, classmates from college, or very close friends. The number will be determined by the size of the wedding, one usher for about every fifty guests. This is his guard of honor, and each must represent the groom as carefully as he would himself. He thinks of these things as he selects them.

That is, he does his best.

He must still be aware—looking deep into his own heart and perhaps into his own immediate past—that these are young and zesty lads fully capable of giving the local police some problems and, even in their most temperate moments, also able to put away more champagne than might be considered possible by even the most openhanded host. He must merely make his choices, and then burn incense on the altar of good hopes. He will not lecture anybody in advance about his responsibilities. He will just pray that fire, mayhem, and wholesale destruction do not visit the area.

The brother of the bride, or a close male relative of hers, will usually be included among the ushers. Former boy friends may be invited as honored guests, but not as ushers.

He buys tokens for his best man and ushers

The groom is expected to supply boutonnieres for his groomsmen, as well as for his father and for his prospective father-in-law. Further than this, it is customary, but not necessary, that he outfit his best man and the ushers with the proper accessories: neckties, or stocks for a formal wedding, gloves, and matching waistcoats.

Whether or not he elects to do all this probably depends upon the relative financial conditions of the groom and his sidekicks. If he has decided upon a formal wedding and is well aware that the requirements of this occasion may strain his ushers' pocketbooks, he may even elect to rent for them the necessary clothing for the occasion. The time is long since past when one has to be afraid of coming upon bullet holes or moth colonies in rented clothing. Formal outfits are now fitted to the special measurements of the groomsmen in advance, and they may arrive looking as if they were turned out freshly by an army of custom clothiers.

The groom should plan to give his best man and his ushers tokens of the occasion, usually some form of jewelry. These usually take the form of cufflinks, miltary brushes, pocketknives, key chains, money-clips, or the like. He endeavors to make his gift to the best man different from the others, and perhaps involving a bit more of an investment.

He instructs the best man and ushers on their duties

The groom must make sure that his team—best man, head usher, and ushers—do him proud. And to do so, they must know the score in advance and coordinate a number of duties which can be done gracefully or awkwardly, or, at the worst, wind up in an awful mess. *Alors:*

His best man serves as ambassador-at-large, roving center, trouble-shooter, and general handyman. He and the bridegroom get together immediately after the engagement is announced and begin to put together their plan of operations.

The best man must assume from the beginning that the groom has taken leave of his senses. He assumes that the happy fellow has now been afflicted by wandering memory, palsied reflexes, drooping of the cortex, wavering of the gray matter affecting decisions, and laid low by a paralysis of spirit and body which leaves him capable only of twitching slightly when poked with a stick.

The best man therefore attacks his duties with brisk dispatch. He keeps checking the groom on everything for weeks. He helps in the selection of ushers, and when the time comes, it is he who organizes them and carries out their operations on suggestions from the groom.

He arranges the bachelor dinner, a bacchanalian rite discussed on page 62. He keeps an ever clear eye on the bridegroom as the wedding day approaches. On the evening before the wedding day, he checks over all the groom's accoutrements, talks to him, soothes him, humors him, and protects him for the great moment. On the day of the wedding, the best man takes on certain matters the groom is almost sure to fumble. He takes possession of the ring. He gets the minister's fee from the groom, and slips it to that reverend gentleman just after the ceremony. The minister has no legal fee, but it is unthinkable to omit it. A proper range is from a minimum of ten dollars up to a hundred, depending upon the size of the wedding and the general relationship of the married couple to the minister, who might well be an old and trusted adviser deserving of a loving gesture. For a small wedding, attended by the family only, a fiver might be permissible, but nothing less will ever be under any circumstances. In any kind of ceremony other than the smallest, the verger will also be on hand, but the bride's family pays him his fee, which is less than the minister's and in proportion.

The best man clings to the groom even more like a leech just before the ceremony. He should anticipate irrational actions now, starts and stops, odd phone calls, and general attacks of apprehension, regret, stage fright, and lassitude. He gets the groom to the church on time, if it takes a club and the fire department combined to do so. They should arrive twenty minutes or a half hour ahead of time. Meanwhile the best man has made sure that the ushers are on hand at the church at least an hour in advance. He arranges with the verger, if the weather makes this necessary, to have the hats and overcoats of the groom and best man handy at the door of the church as they are leaving. The best man helps the groom dress, which the latter seems unable to perform by now. Meanwhile he double-checks a number of points: the groom's travel arrangements, perhaps involving the secreting of at least one car for a getaway after the ceremony, or after the reception if there is one; the safe delivery of the proper flowers to the appropriate people. He makes sure that the bride and groom's luggage is packed and easily available, not omitting to slip a bottle of champagne into the groom's suitcase for that tender first toast with his bride, and other beverages of pleasing flavor if it looks as if they might not be immediately available to the couple as they begin their honeymoon.

During the wedding ceremony itself the best man plays an important part. (We will discuss the ceremony in complete detail later on.) His role is to wait with the groom in the vestry, soothing and pacifying him, while the bride approaches the church. He and the groom then make an inconspicuous entry from the right side of the church and proceed directly to the altar at a signal from the minister, standing slightly to the right as one faces the altar. They turn at the entrance of the bride and observe the bride's procession. The best man watches all this with a pleased expression on his face, but he also keeps an eye on the groom, who may at this moment show symptoms of vertigo, panic, and even faintness. (Brides never have any of this— each one appears smiling and in as complete control of herself as an Academy Award winner.) So the best man stands ready to give the groom both physical and moral support. He has already given the groom the ring, and reminded him twenty times which pocket it is in. Now he murmurs, "Steady, old hoss," or something like that, to prevent a flight from the premises.

After the ceremony is concluded, the bride will leave on the groom's arm, followed by the flower girl. The best man offers his right arm to the maid, or matron, of honor, smiles a magnificent smile, and follows the newly wedded couple out of the church. He may now relax slightly and in a restrained manner smile at those of the guests he knows but has not had an opportunity to greet up until now.

After the wedding there is still no rest for the best man. He is chief traffic officer in directing the guests to the reception. At the bride's table, the best man is toastmaster and he himself gives the first toast to the happy couple, and keeps things moving as the occasion demands. He is a party to the unannounced exit of the bride and groom, and sticks with the groom throughout, making sure that even in the groom's slowly improving state he is still capable of putting his wallet into his jacket, bringing his travel tickets with him, and putting his pants on right side fore when changing into his travel clothes. After the couple has departed into the night and into a new life, the best man sighs with relief, but just before he makes tracks for that girl in the party he hasn't quite found the time as yet to squire as he would like to, he sends a telegram to the parents of the bride in the groom's name, expressing affection and appreciation for the grand and glorious reception.

The ushers have an extremely important role at the wedding and should do it well. The head usher, of course, is their leader. Ideally, he may be the bride's brother or a close relative or friend, and familiar with everyone who will come to the wedding—the members of the family, friends, and special guests. He will be greeting them all as a representative of the bride's family, and if possible he should be a socially inclined, poised, and competent type of fellow who has a pleasant welcome for everyone and a diplomatic way of straightening out every little impasse with complete calm and good humor. It is he who escorts the bride's and the groom's mothers to their respective seats, and escorts both from the ceremony as well. The gentlemen-fathers in each case will permit this honor by following behind, alone, on the entrance; in leaving, the bride will be on her husband's arm and the head usher will again escort the mothers out. He escorts the bride's mother first, and then returns for the groom's mother. She should wait until he thus comes for her, she then leaves on his arm, with her husband following.

The head usher also is responsible for taking care of the ribbon and rug department in the church. It is customary for the special guests at the wedding to be given what amounts to reserved seats in the first rows of the church pews, to whatever number is needed. The head usher has familiarized himself beforehand with the lists of guests and he is quickly aware of who they are as soon as they make their appearance. The reserved seats are indicated by ribbons tied across the pew entrance, off the center aisle. The ushers assist the head usher in the tying and untying of these ribbons: usually it is sufficient to have one or two thus assist the head usher, selecting one of especially pleasing appearance who is not all thumbs at the critical juncture of tying bows or half hitches. The head usher also instructs the ushers in the techniques of removing the white carpet covering from the chancel to the rear of the church. The reason for this covering is to protect the floor of the church itself during the time the guests arrive; after they are all seated, and the bride is ready for her entrance, the ushers roll up the rug, and she walks in all her glory on pristine ground. The ushers must roll the rug carefully, and in concert, so that they do not ram it into a pew with any sidewise swoops and cause any traffic jams holding up the bride. The verger of the church is the best adviser in the matter of how to do this, and where to put the rug after it has been rolled—he's an old hand at this rugged work.

We have suggested one usher for every fifty guests to minimize confusion. These gentlemen array themselves at the entrance of the church and escort each couple as they arrive, each usher offering the lady his right arm, with the escort tagging along behind. If ladies appear together, the usher will offer his right arm to the eldest. The usher endeavors to say a pleasant word or two to each of the guests he escorts, and he invariably asks whether one is a guest of the bride or of the groom: her guests are seated to the left of the church, and the groom's guests to the right, as you face the altar.

We will go into the matter of the bridal procession in considerable detail in describing the bride's and groom's ceremonial responsibilities. The ushers have their own, however. After the bride has entered the church, the ushers form a vanguard and march in a line of twos, each pair about six feet apart. The bridesmaids follow, the maid, or matron, of honor, then the flower girl, and the bride, on the arm of her father. The ushers fan out to the left and right as they reach the altar, leaving room for the main bridal party at the center. At the conclusion of the ceremony the bride leaves the altar with her husband, followed by the flower girl. The best man then follows with the maid of honor, on his right arm. The ushers offer their right arms to the bridesmaids, and exit up the aisle in this order. The head usher leaves the party at the exit and does his stint with the bride's and groom's mothers. After that, the ushers also detach themselves from the bridesmaids—usually with great reluctance—and escort the ladies from among the special guests out of the church. The remainder of the guests have

been held in their places by the strategic ribbons. These are now untied, and all leave the church. The ushers still have social responsibilities. They are expected to be useful as dancing and chatting partners at the reception, with special attention to guests who may seem to be a little out of the festivities. Unmarried ushers will escort unattached bridesmaids, regardless of their charms or lack of them, to the parties in honor of the bride and groom which may follow the reception.

He throws a bachelor dinner

The best time to schedule this time-honored orgy is a few nights before the day of the wedding. The night before is a mistake. Hangovers being what they are, you'll want to look a little better than *that* at your own wedding, and ushers who have to bring collapsible chairs with them in order to rest in the middle of the church aisle from the arduous duties of walking up and down it are somewhat less than efficient, not to say undecorative.

One of the reasons the few-nights-before schedule is a good one is the fact that it will permit you to have out-of-towners present. They simply come in for the wedding a bit early, with a glint in their eye for the magic term "bachelor dinner."

It probably should be a dinner, although it can be just a party if you feel that the mob scene is going to hike the bill too high. *At any rate, don't have it at home!* Have it at your club, if you belong to one, or hire a room in a fashionable restaurant or hotel. They'll take care of all the catering, the checking of hats and coats, and the breakage. Probably you'll want to order steak all around—that's the safest and the most popular—with the usual trimmings.

As we have said, the best man makes the arrangements; the groom pays for the blast. There should be champagne, by all means, at least to the extent of the first toast to the bride. Gallant custom dictates that after the groom has offered his toast to the bride and the champagne is dashed off, the guests break their glasses. A fireplace is a favored receptacle for this devil-may-care gesture: a glass flung across the room and finding the mark with unerring accuracy shatters with a much merrier sound than one merely tapped with the edge of a knife. The best man obviously will have arranged in advance for the champagne glasses to be the best that the ten-cent store or the management can provide at the minimum price and not of the finest crystal. It usually works out that some of the guests are so enchanted at the glass-smashing tradition that they keep it up all night, extending the gesture to the chandeliers, the light bulbs, and frequently their automobiles before the night is over, so that all of the glassware in sight should be strictly of the economy variety.

Men as a rule don't drink too much champagne by preference these days, wanting more substantial beverages, so, after the first toast, the drinking plan should permit more champagne for those who want it, but an open bar with all the works is recommended to get the party under way. The host should anticipate every wish in the drinker's lexicon.

This is the proper time for the groom to distribute his tokens to his groomsmen. The gifts are placed on the table where each man

sits. The evening concludes with a brief and witty speech by the groom-to-be, thanking his cohorts for their presence, their support, and their jolly company, with special reference to his palace guard of groomsmen.

Now, a serious word about the bachelor dinner.

Of course, it's going to be jolly, that's the whole idea. It's probably going to be rough, too. That's par for the course also. And at the end of such revels it is customary for the gang to sally out on the town or to scour the countryside for greener pastures for merrymaking, involving some grandiose concepts in mayhem and highjinks.

After the dinner, after his speech of farewell, the host should vanish. He's done his part. He has shelled out handsomely for as thirsty a set of guzzlers as ever assembled. He has listened with glistening eyes and laughed himself hoarse at various toasts and funny sayings, not to mention the interminable risqué stories which always enrich the atmosphere at such gatherings, until it is quite clear to all that he considers this the greatest concourse of wits and cavaliers that ever graced a groaning board. He has smiled in appreciation to find himself the butt of heavyhanded and suggestive humor, and he has shown himself to be positively delighted at the insults of his closest friends. But he should keep himself in condition to finish off the party on his feet and on his own. He should avoid being delivered to his quarters in a basket, being left in an ash can, or enjoying the hospitality of the local jail for the night. And—to put it bluntly—he should avoid any women. Quite possibly a cake has been served at the banquet from which a beautiful and lively damsel, who forgot to bring any clothes along, may spring and, as previously instructed, head for him like a lemming for the sea. He bears this with fortitude. He smiles fondly at her, indulges in some dignified raillery, and then passes this pastry along to other connoisseurs, eager to oblige his slightest whim. And again, many bachelor dinners wind up with feminine company, sometimes foregathered by great coincidence in one place for the occasion, wherein there may be a plan to involve him with one partner or another, on the fuzzy notion that he deserves some sort of last fling before he takes his vows as a benedict.

The word on this to all grooms: skip it. Tell the boys good night, and don't let them kid you into being a good fellow. You're a good-enough fellow: they're full of *your* food and liquor, and this is your party, not theirs. Let 'em go, bless them all. It will be great hearing about it in the morning. Just don't hang around to watch. There'll be nothing lost in the telling, and there'll be nothing lost—and this is the important point—in the high regard your bride has for you. This is your chance to honor or dishonor her, and there are no if's about it. Don't muff it. End of sermon.

He grooms himself for the wedding

This is a time when every man wants to look his best. It is a time to set aside hardy convictions that the only thing which really counts is an honest heart beating beneath a hairy chest, and subscribe at least for the time being to the feminine dictum that appearances mean practically everything.

Therefore the groom should make himself a private checklist. Haircut a few days before the wedding, not so close to it that he looks shorn or sports a few areas of sunburned skin in contrast to freshly uncovered white, and yet near enough so that his hair remains ruly and exactly at the length in which it appears to best advantage. He should have a watch that runs, a pen that writes, and a pocket-size notebook in which to pen reminders to himself of names, places, and things to do. He might have his nails manicured in the barber shop at the same time—his hands will be critically surveyed by more eyes than he may suspect. If he doesn't want to go to this extent, he should at least cut and file his nails to the best of his own ability, and refrain from tarring roads, painting seachests, digging for clams, or other occupations that may bring him to the altar with blotches or scratches all over his hands.

He should make a special effort to be at his peak in terms of health. This is a good time for a full medical check-up to make sure that all's well in all ways. It is also the time to ease up on certain pursuits that might in any way endanger the success of the wedding.

He might just as well shelve for the time being such adventurous pursuits as skiing, mountain climbing, high diving, drag racing, boxing, or going into cages full of tigers armed only with a chair. A little prudence in this direction will minimize the chances of appearing at the church on crutches, in a wheelchair, or borne on a stretcher.

In the same direction, the groom-to-be might well tone down other excitements, such as barroom argument, staying up all night, or too assiduous drinking of the juices of fermented grains. When these pleasures are reduced to a minimum in the period preceding the wedding, the groom stands a good chance of presenting himself at his physical best. He can, during this period—and you'd be surprised to learn how many young men have done this, myself included—take a special conditioning course at a gym. This will not only build him up to peak condition but will indoctrinate him with certain sound habits and exercise techniques that he may then carry on for the rest of his life, under his own direction.

Similarly, a young man should take stock of himself financially as well as physically. Not everyone can be wealthy when he marries, and very few can be afterward, but the groom should make an effort to put himself into the best position possible at this time. He should have instigated, some time before, a system of regular savings which would bring him into marriage with some kind of backlog down at the bank. He should at this time invest fairly solidly in clothing, which he will need to launch himself into his new career as head of a family. Also, if he can manage it, it would be well for him to enter into matrimony with a new car ready for his bride, or at least one that is in good-enough shape to be of no great concern for some time to come.

It goes without saying that he should be as free as possible of any sizable debts or other encumbrances that it might be unfair to bring into his bride's life. Along the same lines, he should probably work it out so that he is in as advantageous a position as possible in his work. Sometimes a promotion itself suggests that he can now get married. But the least he can do is to be established in a job that he is happy in, in which he sees some chance of advancement, and which in all likelihood will offer him security for some time to come. Part of the same thinking suggests that he now start a program of insurance benefits for his family-to-be, and that he also batten down the hatches against future storms by starting out with hospitalization and accident insurance covering himself and his future family.

Perhaps in seeming contradiction to the above thoughts is the one that if he proposes to make any sizable purchases of a selfish nature— "selfish" in the sense that the contemplated purchase is for himself rather than for him and his bride jointly, such as the acquisition of an expensive shotgun, a set of tools, microscope, or whatnot—such purchase should be made before the marriage and not afterward, since at that time all investments must be considered as a joint venture.

This does not lead to the gruesome conclusion that marriage will forever stand in the way of purchasing shotguns or hifi sets; these are just not sensible purchases to be made in the early years of a marriage, unless the husband is well enough off to handle such extras without interfering with standard household requirements. Similarly, if a young man has a couple of places in the world he wants to visit, he might as well do it now, if it isn't going to eat too deeply into the aforementioned bank account, and get it off his chest once and for all.

He buys his bride a gift

The *meaning* of this gift is our province in this volume, rather than what it should be. It is something a bride will want to treasure forever, and therefore it should be personal, beautiful, and timeless in appeal.

In a word, jewelry.

This is not to squash any impulses on the part of a groom to bestow upon his bride a sportscar, a thoroughbred horse, a pack of hounds, or even a yacht, if his fancy and his means combine to produce such goodies. Even then, however, the sentimental powers of a small bit of jewelry are unequaled at charming the bride. Under such fortuitous circumstances the groom may feel free to proffer both.

One of the finer customs at this time may take the form of presenting the bride with a gift of jewelry that has descended from the groom's family. A necklace, a bracelet, a tiny watch, a ring—these may be enhanced by their age. The groom must have his head about him on this, though: Aunt Agatha's rhinestone stomacher, no matter how strongly advocated by Uncle Olaf or other members of the family, will never do for the bride, nor will the tooth of the Alaskan bear, shot by Grandfather in the Klondike and set in a circlet of gold nuggets, be particularly treasured by a modern young lady. The family treasure must have enduring taste, and manifest value, in order to earn its place as a gift to the bride. The answer may be, sometimes, for the groom to have an antique stone put into a modern setting, or to incorporate a portion of an old cluster of gems into a new cluster surrounding the original.

The gift should be in keeping with the groom's means as well. He wants his bride to treasure it always, but in the meantime he also wants to be able to provide her with food. He will do well to go to a reliable jeweler, one with whom he has already done business, or, lacking that, to the store with the finest reputation, and frankly discuss the problem with them. The amount he spends, what he eventually decides upon, should be a pleasant and loving adventure, filled with the joy of giving.

He coordinates the clothing of the groomsmen

The groom is in on the decision as to whether or not the wedding will be formal. After he has had his say on that, it is up to him to go along with the proper traditions and turn himself out in a manner truly outstanding. His goal should be not to leave any doubt in any guest's mind as to which man is the groom—on appearance alone.

Part of this, of course, is in his "grooming." He should contrive to spend as much as he can on his clothes, having them custom-made for the occasion, in the higher levels of style if they are ready-made, and in all events, crisply new. An exception to this may be in the matter of formal wear. Evening formal calls for a dinner jacket or, in its more formal form, a tailcoat. Daytime formal calls for a cutaway. Now, it may strike a young man that investing in a set of tails or a cutaway is a gesture that will serve him in no sensible way in the future, since he has no knowledge of any future weddings he may attend, and he may be of an age and social position that do not suggest frequent excursions in these garments, if any, in the foreseeable future. If this is the case, he should look into the matter of renting his costume. He should naturally avoid the kind of rental agencies that have a large turnover for freelance waiters or gangster funerals, since bloodstains, gravy discolorations, or bullet holes are going to strike his future parents-in-law and their sharp-eyed allies as somewhat inappropriate. But there are rental agencies that function practically on the level of a custom tailor. They have top-notch garments and, when given plenty of warning, will alter them to fit the man who is going to be in them. This is not always an inexpensive process, but it does come at a lower figure than a full purchase outlay, and a young man should not hesitate to handle the situation this way if the reasons for it are valid.

It is customary for the groom to outfit his best man and his ushers with the proper accessories. However, this is not imperative, as we have said, and probably is something that should be talked over among them in advance. It is usual for the groom to wear a sprig out of the bride's bouquet as his boutonniere. The best man wears a white gardenia. The ushers and the fathers wear white carnations.

His major concern, however, is the apparel itself.

Here is his breakdown. The best man and the ushers follow his lead, with slight variations in accessories.

THE FORMAL DAY WEDDING

The groom wears a black or Oxford-gray cutaway, with striped gray trousers, cuffless. Variation is possible in the waistcoat, which may be of the same material as his jacket, or in white, gray, or buff for contrast. The entire party may wear the same type of waistcoat, or the groom and the best man may wear matching types with the groomsmen wearing another pattern, but with all of theirs matching. His accessories are: white shirt with wing or fold collar, bosom starched or pleated, as desired; ascot tie is the most formal, and usually preferred, although four-in-hand and bow ties are still okay, with the pattern for all in small gray figures, stripes, or checks. He wears black shoes, black socks, and chooses his gloves to harmonize with the waistcoat, in white, gray, or buff. He chooses a white or black pearl stickpin; wears a pocket watch with key chain, if desired; wears formal cufflinks, of gold, pearl, or stone, but inconspicuously sized. Grooms with Service affiliations may find that the gold buttons from their uniforms can be used as uniquely handsome and masculine cufflinks.

The high silk topper is the one to wear for this occasion, although it must be confessed that hats are no longer *de rigueur,* as they used to be. However, leaving the choice up to the groom as to whether he wears a hat or not, if he decides for it, it must be the topper and no other.

If the weather calls for an outer coat, it should be of the formal variety, either single or double breasted, in black, navy blue, or Oxford gray. It is worn with a white or gray muffler.

The groom has the choice of taking a little of the formality off his shoulders by electing to wear the semiformal Oxford gray jacket, and he then carries on with the rest of the formal accessories as outlined above, but never wearing an ascot with this type of jacket. He may wear a black or midnight-blue Homburg hat.

The fathers and ushers will follow suit. Guests may wear the same formal dress if desired, or dark town suits.

THE INFORMAL DAY WEDDING

Here one of the more formal types of town suits will do—black, Oxford gray, medium gray, medium or dark blue. The suit may be single or double breasted. A fine or pin stripe is allowable, but large patterns of colors on the lighter side should be avoided. The trousers, of course, are part of the suit and match the jacket. The groom may wear a vest, but it should go with the suit. Or he may elect to wear no waistcoat. His shirt should be white, with turn-down collar, starched or soft. His tie is a four-in-hand, patterned and colored to harmonize with his suit, a polka dot perhaps, solid navy or black and white in small checks. Black shoes and socks. Homburg or snapbrim felt, and straw hats in season. He should wear gloves, preferably gray or buff. Topcoat and muffler, regular town wear, preferably on the dark side. Fathers, ushers, and guests in dark town suits.

THE FORMAL EVENING WEDDING

The groom wears midnight-blue or black tailcoat, trousers in the same fabric as the coat with double-braided sides, single- or double-breasted waistcoat in white piqué, V front. Starched-front shirt, with bold wing collar, and white piqué bow tie. Patent-leather shoes or pumps, with black silk socks. White gloves, pearl or precious-stone studs, with cufflinks to match. Watch and key chain are permissible. He wears a silk topper or collapsible opera hat, with formal topcoat in black, dark blue, or gray. Fathers, ushers, and guests wear the same.

THE SEMIFORMAL EVENING WEDDING

The groom shifts to the dinner jacket ensemble. It is black or midnight blue, shawl collar and single breasted, and with it he wears a black or midnight-blue cummerbund, white shirt with fold or wing collar, black or midnight-blue bow tie, patent-leather pumps or shoes (regular black or even suede is permissible), gray gloves, gray pearl studs. Black or midnight-blue Homburg, with formal topcoat, white scarf. Ushers, fathers, and guests also wear dinner jackets.

THE INFORMAL EVENING WEDDING

The groom wears a dark town suit, a white shirt, and chooses his accessories to strike a formal note: white shirt with turn-down collar, stiff or soft, gray figured four-in-hand tie, or small black-and-white or blue-and-white checks. Black shoes are a must: brown isn't ever permissible. Dark socks to harmonize with suit. Dark blue or black hat. Fathers, ushers, and guests wear the same.

THE SUMMER EVENING WEDDING

For this wedding the semiformal rules apply, summer style. The jacket is of lightweight material, single or double breasted; the trousers remain dark, in black or midnight-blue lightweight material. The shirt is white, again, but the tie and cummerbund set may be in maroon, black, midnight blue, or in the various formalized patterns utilizing several colors. Black patent-leather pumps or shoes, studs and cufflinks as usual. A lightweight straw hat adds a nice touch. Fathers, ushers, and guests wear the same.

THE GARDEN WEDDING

The men relax in jackets and slacks, with the jackets in navy blue, blue-gray, gray, or small patterns, if any (avoid the horsy-set look with country checks or large figures), and contrast these with their slacks, in white, gray, or harmonizing tones of blue or tan. All-white suits or regular summer-weight suits of a formal pattern are permissible. The shirts should always be white, but the tie may range in any sensible and harmonizing colors and patterns, either four-in-hand or bow. The rules are off on shoes: they may be black, white, brown, or even in moccasin styles. The only thing to avoid here is an obviously sporty shoe: perhaps the way to solve it is to skip any possible style with rubber or crepe soles, and stick to those with leather soles and heels. Fathers, ushers, and guests, of course, follow suit. Here again, a straw is permissible, and a good idea is to have all the men of the bridal party wear skimmers with matching bands.

He perfects his wedding etiquette

The groom actually has the easiest role of all to play, and that is the very reason why he should have it letter-perfect in his mind. First, he gets his flower orders in order:

The groom supplies boutonnieres for the groomsmen, for his father, and for his prospective father-in-law.

He pays for the bride's bouquet, which she, however, usually selects. He also buys corsages for the bride's mother and his own.

The groom also pays the clergyman's fee. This should be in new bills or a check, and should be put into an envelope which the best man will give to the clergyman after the ceremony. It is none of the best man's business what the size of the fee will be.

FOR THE CEREMONY

At the wedding ceremony the groom is above all expected to arrive on time. As we have noted, he is pretty much in the hands of his best man, and doesn't have to do much except go along with the tide. A word about drinking at this point. The best plan is not to drink at all. Of course, there'll be plenty of time for that later, in the traditional toasting of the bride and wedding couple, and at the reception. But if

just now the groom feels that he needs a little bucking up for the ordeal ahead, he must still realize that he is in a very nervous and tense condition and that any liquor is going to hit him harder than it usually does. So for the sake of appearing at his best, and behaving at his best, he should keep his prenuptial quaffs to a minimum or have them not at all.

Groom and best man arrive at the church at least twenty minutes before the hour set for the wedding. They wait, chafing at the bit, in the vestry until they receive word that the bride has arrived at the church. The groom keeps calm at this point. All he has to do is follow the clergyman into the chancel, coming in from the side, and accompanied by his best man. At a formal wedding, the groom will be wearing gloves, and he removes the right one before he goes out to meet his bride. If it is to be a double-ring ceremony, he removes both, and gives them to the best man for safekeeping until after the ceremony. His top hat, if he is wearing one, and his cane, if he is sporting one, are left in the vestry. The best man gets them immediately after the ceremony and hustles them around to the church entrance, with his coat if that is in season, and gives them to him just before he and the bride leave the church.

At the end of the ceremony, it is customary for the groom to kiss the bride. This is a token kiss, and he does it with dignity and not as if he is starring in a movie close-up.

From here on out, all that the groom has to remember is to keep the bride always on his right. After the ceremony is completed, he turns and gives her his right arm, and they proceed down the aisle in that position. She should also be on his right in the car driving to the reception.

FOR THE RECEPTION

In the reception line he stands third in line, with his bride on his right. (First in line is the bride's mother, as hostess, then the groom's mother, and then the groom's father. The bride's father may, of course, feel that he may be needed at the head of the line in order to introduce business acquaintances and others who might not be known even to his wife. But usually he will circulate and get the party started happily as the guests pass through the line.)

The groom merely smiles and thanks the guests for their good wishes. However, he is in a favorable position to introduce his bride to any of his own friends and guests who may come along, and whom she may not have met previously. The introduction follows the usual form.

AT THE WEDDING TABLE

After the last guest has been received, the bridal party is seated at their table. The bride sits at the groom's right, with the best man at her right and the maid of honor at the groom's left. The bridesmaids and ushers then dispose themselves alternately around the table. Special-guest couples, and the husbands of bridesmaids and wives of ushers, are also included.

Then on comes the champagne. The bride's glass is filled first, then the groom's, and so on around the table. This leaves the best man to be served last. When his glass is filled, he rises and proposes the first toast to the bridal couple. After this toast, the groom toasts his bride, and from then on it's every man for himself in the inspiration of toasts. Meanwhile, the best man regales the company by reading aloud telegrams and letters that have been sent to the bride's home and the reception.

After the main course has been served, the bride and groom together cut the wedding cake, each placing the right hand on the same knife. They share the first piece of cake together, in symbolism of their troth. After that, the rest of the cake is cut and served to the guests by the waiters.

IF THERE'S DANCING

At a large reception, there will usually be music, and if there's music, there should be dancing. In that case the bride and groom always dance together for the first number, alone. The bride's father cuts in on the groom after a short interval, followed by the groom's father, the best man, and then the ushers, in that order. The groom, meanwhile, goes on his way to dance his second dance with the bride's mother, and follows that by dancing with his own mother. He also makes sure that at some time during the festivities he dances at least once with the matron of honor and each of the bridesmaids.

BEFORE THE TRIP

When the party is in full swing, although they may be enjoying themselves tremendously, the bridal couple should make plans for their departure. The groom slips away to a room which has been reserved for his use and changes into his travel clothes. His bag has already been packed, thanks to the best man, and also thanks to that hard-working individual, the rest of the couple's luggage has been stowed in their car, or is already at the station, airport, dock, or nearby hotel if they plan to spend their first night together in the vicinity before embarking on their honeymoon.

When the bride emerges in her travel costume, the bride and groom then make their farewell appearance, bid their adieus, and depart for their life together as the party goes on in their absence.

The groom keeps in mind the thoughtfulness of others in providing such a festive occasion. A telegram is sent in his name by the best man to the parents of the bride, thanking them for the reception. But he should also send the bride's parents a special note informing them of the newlyweds' safe arrival at the honeymoon destination. Besides this, he should also send a courteous note of appreciation to the clergyman who launched them on their life together.

The wedding is over: his career as head of the family has begun.

He plans the honeymoon

The honeymoon is up to the groom. He pays for it, he makes his arrangements in plenty of time, he sees to it that it becomes one of the greatest experiences of their lives together.

To begin with, he should talk over the whole idea of the honeymoon with his bride-to-be. There are all sorts of honeymoons, of course, and he now has to start being considerate of his wife's wishes in the matter.

If he is an expert golfer and thinks that making the grand tour of all the links is the perfect honeymoon, he might stop to think a bit and perhaps learn that his bride-to-be has been dreaming of a tour reaching all of the famous art galleries. If he is a mountain climber and has always cherished the dream of climbing an entire range at one fell swoop, perhaps his little sweetheart is not half as enamored of felling and swooping as he, and possibly even not up to it physically. This type of careful investigation should go into all of the couple's interests, be they in Eskimo culture, winter training camps of baseball teams, fishing, collecting trivets, visiting old college scenes or old college chums.

Sometimes a chance stroke of luck may decide everything. When we were married, it was entirely the custom to go either to Bermuda or Sea Island. It still is, of course, and eminently a good one. But we did not have a lot of time for our honeymoon; besides, there had been enough of a social whirl before the wedding to make it important that our honeymoon really get us away from it all. One of our friends suggested that we take over his summer home on Martha's Vineyard. A mild storm of protest arose over this. An island off the North Atlantic in *November?* Who ever heard of Martha's Vineyard? In fact, at that time not many people had. Its charming secrets were being kept from the public interest by a conspiracy of its sparse population, consisting of old island families reaching back to the very model of Captain Ahab himself among the whaling set, Indians who are still there today, and a few lucky artists and lovers of quietude such as my friend, who had discovered the rare retreat and had by good behavior been accepted as part of the insular family. But we went to the Vineyard anyway, and our reward was heavenly. The "cottage" had been so described, in the old New England fashion, which designates any structure in a resort as a "cottage" be it ever so humbly the address of forty rooms and riding stables. This was not of that type of Newport grandeur, but it had a grandeur of its own, made of huge fireplaces, four-poster beds, views of the sea from the shaded street on which it stood, the quietness of autumn nights in Vineyard Haven, and the added blessing of an Indian summer during every hour of our honeymoon, which bathed it in a golden haze while we were there. The glow persists in our memories until this minute.

This reminiscence is not for the sake of mere sentimentality so much as to illustrate that the Vineyard was indeed better than the standard resort for our special and personal tastes. It so happened that we were fond of strolling through old graveyards, where the names rang like a roll call of all the whaling captains on the sea, of chatting with the Indians and watching them at their pottery, of fishing and swimming in the still warm sea, and walking for miles on clean beaches without ever encountering anything but nature itself. Another couple might find this disappointingly uneventful and prefer a motor trip from one entertaining resort to another, or perhaps a trip to the end of the world, to satisfy a dream with the reality of a tinkling temple bell, a lagoon murmuring in the moonlight, or a jungle trail leading to unexpected Edens. Since these images can by some strange alchemy of love be applied to anywhere a wedded couple may go, the Vineyard or Zamboanga, we shall let each honeymooner find out the secrets, with only the guiding thought that this is the most important trip they will ever take together or separately. The trip may be to a country inn for a weekend only, or for a month in a foreign city. No matter. It is all one if it has been chosen affectionately and well.

If the wedding trip is not to be taken by motor to a spot nearby, the chances are that it will be made by air. Most honeymooners today have wings, which brings the world to them in only a matter of hours. Seven days spell a honeymoon in Nassau, Bermuda, Jamaica, or other calypso lands of the Caribbean. Eleven days will reach to Panama, Quito, and Lima. Two weeks is enough to take in Europe. Thirty days will take your dream around the world.

Not that traveling by sea has become obsolete. Far from it. Honeymooners having a day or two more than a week may enjoy a leisurely trip aboard ship and the fun of setting foot on foreign soil. Cruises that visit three ports of the West Indies, with time ashore for exploring the islands, take eleven days. In thirteen days another cruise visits four ports. Nassau, Jamaica, and Bermuda can be managed within seven or eight days afloat. Cruises to Europe or North Africa with ample time on land are available in four to six weeks of easy travel by sea.

The best time for the groom to start planning the honeymoon is the day of his engagement. There are thousands of places to consider, and several will no doubt look as good as another, necessitating some decision-making before the die is cast. The season of your wedding date will influence you greatly, of course; but there will be plenty of places to chose from. California, Florida, and the Southwest offer year-round attractions. Sun Valley, Aspen, Stowe, and other ski areas offer as much color and romance in the winter as in the summer. Of the national parks the south rim of the Yosemite and Grand Canyon may be visited at any time, but the summer bride should keep in mind that the national parks close around the middle of September. The West Indies, Bermuda, Nassau, and Mexico are fine throughout the entire calendar year.

Summer brides may be escorted to such far-flung spots as Alaska, Guatemala, and Haiti. With a little over five weeks available, a visit to Hawaii is a romantic tour, with a swing on to half a dozen islands of the South Pacific, with stops at such storied ports as Honolulu, Pagopago, Suva, Auckland, Wellington, Sydney, Papeete, and back to the lively ports of San Francisco and Los Angeles.

A hop skip and a jump away are nearer resorts which may not have the romance in their names of a Bangkok or a Palawan, but they furnish luxurious and gay hotels, many of them with special accommodations for honeymooners. The White Mountains, the Adirondacks, the Poconos, the lake country of Minnesota and Wisconsin, all abound in engaging retreats. Then there are the Laurentians, the Green Mountains of Vermont, and the Canadian lakelands. For brides and grooms of the Mississippi Valley, the Canadian Rockies are not too far.

There are music and dance festivals in all parts of the country to which you may want to key the honeymoon; there are skiing festivals; there's basking on some southern beach along the coastline, and skin diving for the nonsnoozers. There are more islands like Martha's Vineyard; there are hidden hamlets in the countryside; there are mountain retreats. It is a good idea to talk to as many people as you can in an effort to discover the most exciting idea of all for you and your bride. Then, if the trip you have decided upon becomes more than a matter of a few phone calls and a letter or two, you surely should look up a reliable travel agent and take advantage of the really remarkable and valuable services the people can offer you. They wrap up practically every aspect of your trip, get all the tickets, arrange for all the accommodations, set the whole itinerary, and advise you completely, on the basis of close personal contacts and experience in all parts of the world.

Here are a few important things to remember while preparing your honeymoon plans:

1. Explore the facts and figures of reduced fare for midweek travel

on the airlines. A man and his wife traveling together may find the savings enough to go first-class instead of air coach.

2. Make that forty-four pounds air coach, sixty-six pounds first-class, count in packing for the nuptial flight. Buy strong luggage of maximum capacity, minimum weight.

3. Assemble your wardrobe to fit exactly the needs of your wedding trip. In summer, count on wrinkle-proof, drip-dry fabrics for you both. Plan for sports and sightseeing and nights of dancing, whether on a tropic isle, European cobblestones, or snowy ski slopes and after-ski evenings. *Note:* the groom should take it easy on the number of shoes *he* takes. Four pairs of brogans, size somewhere around eleven, can weigh as much as a girl's whole wardrobe.

4. Remember that tours are not necessarily planned for groups. They can easily be keyed to travel for two.

5. Remember that when you are returning from foreign travel you are allowed to bring merchandise for personal use worth $100 free of duty. This regulation applies to each returning resident of the United States whether he is a citizen or not.

6. No passports are required for Americans honeymooning in Canada, Mexico, Central America, Bermuda, Nassau, the West Indies, Hawaii, or Alaska.

He lends a thought to luggage

The luggage of a honeymooning couple does get quite a complete looking over, and certainly it is as personal as a calling card. It should not be casually or hastily chosen. The idea is to assemble a collection of luggage that will be useful in the future—the man will, for instance, probably need some large units for business trips, and the girl will want something handy for overnight or weekend jaunts—but at the same time a distinguished unity should be sought rather than just a collection of odds and ends. Matched cases look particularly well, and will, after the honeymoon, look well on vacations. The new cases should be considered for lightness and strength, and can be of the kind that are fashioned into sizes which nest one inside the other for home storage. And you should keep in mind the double-duty functions of so much modern luggage: cases with hanging arrangements that are removable, or shoe bags whose compartments can be taken out, and the case crammed with extras.

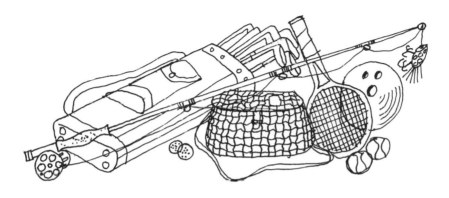

Co-educational luggage, as they say (they couldn't call it bisexual), calls for a meeting of minds on color. Most men prefer tan, while most girls prefer navy-blue, white, or red bindings on their luggage, or perhaps she goes for plaids. If they can't settle on a common color or design, they still can buy their luggage consistently—with all of his in one color, and hers in the one she prefers. That might even be useful in recognizing the units when they are delivered en masse to the hotel room or cabana.

The bride's luggage is really part of her trousseau and will be taken up in the next "her" section. As for him, the basic luggage for a groom should primarily consist of a two-suiter—a case that will actually hold three suits if one of them is of tropic weight, as a dinner coat and trousers, for example. This case will not only hold the suits, but the shirts, ties, and other gear a man needs to go with them. In addition to it, he will need an overnight case, and this should not be less than twenty-one inches. With these two cases, it is possible to provide for a two-week trip.

Don't be timid about tossing some really utilitarian pieces in with your honeymoon luggage. No one need be ashamed of a duffel bag, stuffed with the kind of useful things that just don't belong in a suitcase. Kit bags, gladstone cases, and club bags all have their adherents. The kit bag especially possesses loyal admirers among travelers whose helter-skelter packing habits are admirably served by this ugly but useful kind of luggage. But the flight bag developed from the B-4 of wartime years has partisans, who find that its hanging space teamed with pockets for other clothing, in addition to its being so easily stowable, suits them perfectly.

She plans everything in conference with her family

This is a time when no one can afford to rush into things, to make premature announcements or even act on decisions that may have to be changed later.

Now is the time for an inner-inner conference. First, there should be a meeting of the young couple with the bride-to-be's parents. The time of the wedding is decided, and different suggestions taken up and discarded until a complete harmony of idea and plan is achieved. From here on, this is the inner group which must function as one in purpose and accord, so the very first thing is to have an absolute understanding about everything.

The final decision is now made as to the nature of the wedding, whether it is to be strictly formal or not and, in general, how large it is to be, because these are basic decisions that will affect so much of the bride's subsequent planning.

Once the strategic plan has been set, it is now time to get into the operational phases. And the first, and perhaps most important move of all, is when?

She selects her bridal gown and accessories

For all present, family and guests, the visual summing up of the entire wedding is the costume of the bride. It is the thing that draws all eyes as she moves up the aisle on the arm of her father. She is the star, and since she at all times holds the center of the scene, it is imperative that her costume be one that shows her at her loveliest best. Moreover, it is the thing her memory will treasure most.

By far the most critical choice a bride-elect is called upon to make is the selection of her wedding costume. Having already determined whether her wedding is to be formal or informal, she turns to fashion and fabric to attain the vision of beauteous perfection she sees in her dreams. The fashion she selects should be the one most effective for her type, and the fabric must be becoming, so that together they create the ideal bridal picture. It somehow happens that most brides are beautiful on their wedding day. This may be partly because of their special radiance at this high moment, but it can also be true that for the first time in her life many a girl has given real thought to what she is going to wear and achieves a unity that in itself is a triumph.

The wedding costume is always foremost in the thoughts of a girl about to be married. While she is arriving at a choice, it is a time for her to regard herself critically and consider her height, her waistline, and her coloring. It is a time for discrimination and weighing of values. It is a convention that the full-skirted wedding gown is becoming to almost all types of girl, short, tall, plump, slim. But the bride's own type has much to do with the cut of the bouffant gown she decides on. A tiny bride who is a trim five feet four inches, including heels, should have a dress that, though its skirt be full, should be made of one fabric, with its fullness beginning a little below the waistline. The basque is a demure example of this style, with the long torso so becoming to a small girl. It is important that there are no crosslines to cut her height, though if all details are in proportion, quite elaborate decoration may be used, such as the tiny tucking, braids, buttons and bows, and even the flower-decked flounces found on the wedding dresses of Victorian brides. The petite bride dressed with care presents a charming picture. The girl who is five feet eight inches, with or without heels, can wear very definite lines. Her skirt may be extravagantly full and billowy like a Winterhalter beauty, or she may have very slim lines giving her an elongated look, effective for tall girls unless they are excessively thin. *Note:* The tall bride whose dress is slim should select wide-skirted frocks for her attendants as a foil for her slimness.

The fortunate girl of medium height, around five feet six inches in heels, can wear almost any type of dress. She may choose from many of the fashions becoming to her tall or tiny sister.

Naturalness is the ideal to be sought in the wedding costume. Veil and gown should clothe the bride with natural grace and ease as much as with style and exquisite fabric. Guard against overstaging. No bride needs or should strive to step out of an exotic fashion magazine. This does not demand simplicity, but rather what harmonizes with the personality of the bride. Above all in the bridal scene as she moves toward the altar, she should be herself, a readily recognizable glorification of herself.

Her veil or headdress should accentuate the personality of the bride along with the becomingness of her gown. To achieve this ideal result, she must first decide how she will wear her hair and, once that is settled, not change it after she has chosen her headdress. It is no time to pick a startlingly different coiffure regardless of how à la mode it may be. If a girl is the slim American beauty with a touch of the outdoors about her and has a longish bob, she should keep it that way. Her hair may be shaped and trimmed, but not changed to what may prove an incongruous style.

Points to consider once the bridal gown is chosen, and her coiffure settled, are her height, her coloring, and the shape of her face. For instance, the bride with the rare and charming heart-shaped face is not at her best under a coronet, no matter how much she may fancy it. She may wear an interesting bow, or one of the versions of the appealingly simple little cap of Juliet. The coronet or tiara is best on a bride with regular features, and even then it should be scaled down, for a bride should not look majestic but dainty and winning. A tiara is charming if tiny and not top-heavy. The tiny tiara is young; a high one isn't. With dark skin the color of a veil must not be stark white, but an off shade or an ivory tone.

The type of bridal gown chosen is important in deciding the length of the bridal veil, and brides today should be happy that the old veil of many layers extending not less than eighteen inches beyond the train of the wedding dress, overpowering to a young bride, is well out of fashion. Instead the effect is always airy, always young. A modern bride may wear a veil over her face; it has a beguiling maidenly look particularly apt for a bride. Generally speaking, whether the veil is worn over the face or not, its shape is irregular, short at the sides, longer in back, and proportioned to the height of the bride and the length of her dress, but always airy and filmy.

FORMAL BRIDAL GOWN

Though the long train inevitably indicates a formal wedding, a superb dress of high fashion that comes barely to the floor may be equally formal and call for full formality in the treatment of clothes for the bridal party, especially of the men. Very formal in feeling is the dress with long sleeves and high neck when made of luxurious fabric, but a simply cut gown with a short train—often termed chapel length—indicates a wedding of less formality.

Fashions in necklines vary little from season to season. The sweetheart, cut vaguely like a heart and considered especially appropriate to brides, the portrait neckline, and one off the shoulders are favorite fashions of every season. Experts in bridal salons are ingenious, and if a girl who still shows signs of adolescent thinness wants a dress with these pretty necklines, they may be filled in with yokes of bridal illusion with no loss in effect. But high, low, square, round, or off the shoulders, the neckline must be inspected carefully for becomingness before a well-lighted mirror.

FABRICS KEYED TO TIME OF YEAR

Fabrics are keyed to the season of the year, though it is worth noting that many of them are right for any season. Lace, tulle, taffeta, peau de soie, and the almost indestructible nylon net are all-year fabrics. Silk organza may be added to brocade, velvet, moire, faille, and bengaline for winter. Fine cotton organdy, embroidered or plain, is worn only in summer. Laces for winter are heavy, often re-embroidered or sprinkled with paillettes; examples are heavy cord lace and guipure. Summer laces are airy, with Chantilly and Alençon leading the field. The beloved classic, white satin, is at its best in the fall-winter-spring cycle.

HER CROWNING BEAUTY, THE BRIDAL VEIL

The bride's headdress is the symbol of the wedding, and exclusive to it. By ancient custom it bespeaks the entire pageant and ceremony. As much as the gown, and perhaps more, it imparts identity and individuality to the bride. It is the crowning beauty of the wedding costume.

The wedding veil of family lace, worn by several generations of brides, may be exquisitely beautiful, or all wrong. Whether or not to use one is a decision hard to make, for sentiment has much to do with it; but it's a decision that must be faced up to by one bride or another in a family. If the lace has been well kept and has become a pale, unspotted ivory, it may be becomingly worn by a bride no matter how young, but to look its best it must preserve the desirable airy effect by being placed over tulle. Furthermore, it must be attached to a foundation cap that will stay firmly in place; and finally, if it is a big veil of heavy lace, it should not be considered for the tiny bride, no matter how deep its tradition within the family. Worn with grace by a bride of sufficient height, it may be magnificent; but no bride on this happy day should wear it simply because it is a family heirloom.

The variety of headdresses topping the veil is so wide that every bride is sure of finding one both becoming and individual. Bows, for instance, are made in many versions, all especially suitable to young brides. They may be of the type Goya loved to paint, with floating ends; they may derive from the Alsacienne's regional costume, the bow broad and flat; they may be wide or narrow, of satin or velvet, taffeta or organdy, of ribbon or lace. They are all becoming to most brides. If a bow is chosen by the bride, her attendants will also be topknotted with bows. If the bride likes the idea of a crown, she may wear, instead of a tiara, a little wreath of flowers, which may give the effect of a tight Della Robbia garland.

Whatever flowers make up the bridal headdress are also used in the bridal bouquet. They are always the flowers the bride loves best. White roses, lilacs, hyacinths, orange blossoms—all the flowers of spring and high summer are effective.

For a garden wedding, with the bride attired in billowy ballerina-length bridal gown, a big flower-laden picture hat is bridal and beautiful. With frothy white lilacs for bouquet and hat, the picture is breath-taking. When the bride wears a hat, attendants wear big leghorns with streamers.

Tight little caps, shallow and plain, made of the fabric of the wedding dress, or of lace or tulle, becoming to all brides, are as delicate as a flower petal, and hold a veil elegantly. They are never constructed to resemble a hat.

The bride everywhere is fortunate in having these and many other headdresses from which to choose the best to present her at her prettiest. As she steps forward on the arm of her father, it will be the symbol of her wedding.

BRIDAL MAKE-UP

Make-up, always sparing and understated on a bride, may nevertheless be a help in counteracting stark-white; but it is intelligent to select an off shade of white fabric, such as pale ivory, which may be kind to a less than perfect skin, and there are many of these off-white shades that have the pristine beauty of white together with becomingness. *Note:* The bride is well advised to have professional advice on make-up for her wedding, with a sample of the white as a guide.

JEWELRY FOR THE BRIDE

Every bride wishes to wear the jewel her groom may have given her, and the chances are very good that it will present no problem. A cross or circlet of pearls or diamonds may be appealing worn on a slender chain. And nearly every bride with a low or slightly cutout neckline will find a string of smallish pearls becoming, but she must avoid all heavy costume jewelry, even though it may be made of gold. Much delicate costume jewelry, copied from exquisite originals, is charming with bridal white, but it must be chosen with caution. Occasionally an elaborate set of family jewelry, including a pair of bracelets, a necklace, and earrings, may be given a bride to wear on her wedding day; but it poses a real problem, one to be considered with great care in deciding the fabric and fashion of her wedding gown. Today's bride faces this problem less frequently than did her Victorian great-grandmama. Nevertheless, Victorian jewelry of gold with turquoise or pearl settings can be charming with a sweetheart or portrait neckline.

BRIDAL ACCESSORIES

Slippers to go with her wedding dress should be simple pumps made of the fabric of her dress, or of white satin with a tiny bow, beading, or a small cluster of orange blossoms or lilies of the valley with a lace rosette. If she is to have a large wedding reception and must stand for an hour or more, she should choose baby french heels for her comfort's sake as well as for their own charm. Stockings should be of a nude shade close to the color of her skin or, as many fashionable brides decide, white hose, very fetching beneath her bridal white gown. As to gloves, she may wear them if she wishes, but they are not strictly necessary. With short sleeves long gloves may be very beautiful, but be warned that the seam of the ring finger must be ripped so that the covering may be whipped off the finger at that important moment in the ceremony.

Part of the bride's trousseau will be her honeymoon luggage. She will probably want matched luggage, although it is not entirely necessary that her own luggage match her husband's pieces. She should start with a twenty-one-inch case, and, together with a Pullman case, this will afford her a dozen changes. The car sack, which she may carry instead of a Pullman case, or in addition to it, will hold dresses reasonably free from wrinkles. A Mayfair case or bottle box for toiletries will have either a mirror in the top or a removable easel back mirror. It is at its best if it is large enough to hold night clothes and a pair of soft slippers. Having it available for freshening up en route makes more sense than depending upon a compact and package of tissues in a handbag. When the honeymoon trip is made by car, the lightweight shoe bag which holds six pairs takes the strain off the other cases.

A lightweight hatbox, of which there are countless types to match any series of luggage, is endlessly useful. Nearly always made with pockets in the sides and top, it will accommodate stockings, handkerchiefs, and so on, as well as the hats it was made for.

She coordinates clothes of bridal party and attendants

An effective idea many brides have successfully adopted is to have all gowns of the bridesmaids in one basic color, with tones of the color used for costumes of the maid of honor and mothers of bride and groom; a truly glamorous effect when beautifully carried out.

The following chart, based on pink, illustrates the values of a color, keyed to basic pastel colors. Pale blue may move to deep sapphire; green may shade to emerald; mauve to deep purple and grape; pale yellow to deep gold and topaz.

> COLOR CHART FOR BRIDAL PARTY, BASED ON PINK
> Maid of Honor: *Fuchsia*
> Bridesmaids: *Pale Pink*
> Flower Girl: *White-Pink Flowers Carried*
> Mother of Bride: *Ruby*
> Mother of Groom: *Cherry*

DRESSES OF BRIDAL ATTENDANTS

The dresses of her attendants, which are always keyed to her costume, obey rather strict tradition. As foil for the bride, whoever is directing the production—usually the girl herself, with help from her mother and/or a bridal consultant—picks pattern and fabric that build up the scene. This means that for formal or informal weddings, with the bride in white, silk is worn with silk, cotton with cotton, and the style is selected to dramatize the bride. This may sometimes be gained, as indicated before, by bouffant dresses for her maids when the bride wears a slimly cut gown.

If there is a pair of junior bridesmaids, dresses duplicate basically those of the other maids. When there is a single junior bridesmaid, her dress may be of slightly different fashion, her low-heeled shoes probably of satin dyed to match her frock.

After having viewed the entire range of fashion and fabric and color, we must leave a final thought: It is that the bride in white is still supreme, and she is the overwhelming choice of grooms.

She starts her personal and household trousseau

Trousseau time is the one time in the life of a girl when she may spend freely up to the last dollar with a clear conscience. It is also probably the first time in her life that she sets out seriously to assemble her clothes as a properly organized whole and achieves that perfectionistic triumph, a total wardrobe.

In pre-engagement years, a girl has lightheartedly bought a dress when she saw one she liked, at times extravagantly. She bought lingerie in the same casual way, as she needed it, or as a piece of feminine frippery that caught her fancy. But from the moment a bride-to-be begins to compile the first tentative lists for invitations and announcements her trousseau becomes a challenge to acquire all the pretty things she has yearned to own.

It is the part of wisdom as well as the human thing for a girl to start planning her trousseau with her honeymoon in close view, but coordinating it with her permanent wardrobe.

Plan a trousseau first for the honeymoon, keying your purchases to

where and how you will live the first year. A bride who will continue a business career will obviously not need the same wardrobe as the girl who will be a housewife only. As a first step, once the honeymoon spot is decided on, make a list of what you will specifically need for it; then pick out things that will integrate with your post-honeymoon wardrobe.

Make preliminary selections the minute the wedding dress has been chosen, especially the going-away outfit. It should be a dress or suit, to be worn over and over again later. Incidentally, the mode of honeymoon travel will influence the type of suit needed for it. For a motor trip a good-looking flannel or tweed skirt worn with a pullover and/or cardigan is practical and smart; for taking off by train, plane, or on a cruise, a wool suit in winter, a light, crease-resistant suit made of a blend of synthetic and natural fibers in summer.

Further down-to-earth advice: Dispassionately consider your present wardrobe—what can be repaired, cleaned, restyled to fit without a wrinkle into your trousseau. A surprising amount can be salvaged, but everything must be spanking fresh, including scarves, gloves, and handbags. Take a full day for this job. You'll need it.

No two women's wardrobes can be identical, no matter how similar their incomes, or even their jobs. (And that's all for the best.) But every woman should have a good suit, a simple day dress to wear with furs or under a coat. It should be one that can be dressed up or down by the accessories she puts with it, with good costume or real jewels. She also needs a short dinner dress, of a sort that may be worn to a cocktail party with a headdress of flowers, or a bow and veil, and two or three hats, for even when a girl likes the hatless idea, there are times when her costume needs the finish of a hat. The hats must be just as carefully chosen as everything else.

LINGERIE

It is wise to have lingerie of one color and, for the most part, things that one can launder in a wash basin, especially when traveling. She should own a minimum of two girdles; no girl can readily do without them. Panties, bra, and slip should match girdles in color, and in traveling with light and dark clothes, one set of light, one set of dark, underwear should be packed. A dark bra should go under dark sweaters.

Beyond the lingerie that goes under her clothes, no woman needs a list, for every woman has her own ideas of what she needs, and most brides need no urging to splurge on these enchanting imponderables.

A classic, warm dressing gown, possibly pale blue or yellow, instead of schoolgirl navy blue or plaid, gains importance by having a monogram on the collar point, breast pocket, or on the sleeve above the cuff. And a pretty negligee for bedroom use only is practical luxury if it is made of nylon.

Girls getting married today must shape the traditional trousseau to fast-moving times. Recall what happens in women's fashions—changing silhouettes and hemlines—and regardless of the money you have to spend, avoid lingerie on too grand a scale. A billowing petticoat today will probably give way to a pencil-slim slip tomorrow.

SEPARATES' PLACE IN THE TROUSSEAU

Separates are international. Starting with practical sweaters and skirts, they now embrace every facet of dressing and fashion, with the exception of the grand ball gown. They are worn by smart women everywhere, in Paris, London, and New York, and from coast to coast. For practical wardrobe building they are better than diamonds as a girl's best friend. First, of course, a variety of sweaters, to be added to whenever possible; slim skirts and wide skirts, for night and day; jackets that may be teamed with different skirts for a change of pace. But separates should be bought to plan, so that different colors blend, not clash, and so that they fit in with accessories happily. Knit skirts, either by machine or clever fingers, are practical. With a skirt of navy blue, for instance, a matching jacket may be worn as well as one of navy blue and white for a completely different look; and this scheme may be carried through with brown, gray, or any favorite basic color. Coordination is the word and idea that brings them all together harmoniously.

SHOES AND ACCESSORIES

Shoes are likely to use up a great deal of the trousseau money, but they are a feminine extravagance every woman understands. Well-shod feet are as important to a woman's appearance as her grooming.

It is important to have the best shoes she can afford and for them to fit perfectly. It is safer to buy fewer, rather than half a dozen pairs of lesser quality. A pair of multicolor pumps, perhaps flowered ones, will go with several dresses of different colors. Patent-leather pumps are fine in spring with print dresses, as well as with blue or black, and they are a chic accent with brown. Three pairs of day shoes are the least a woman can do with, and at least one pair should have a medium heel to wear with tweeds, or in town for shopping.

Extra hats, shoes, gloves, hand bags for day or evening, bought as one can afford, extend the scope of a wardrobe. For permanent usefulness two daytime bags are necessary; one of leather to go with a variety of things, and a smaller one of suede or fabric for formal day wear. A small evening bag made of brocade or bright silk, or beaded with pearl or white, should be large enough to carry lipstick and powder, a handkerchief, and a little purse for change, keys, and a bill or two. Wash gloves of fabric, leather, or string crochet for daily wear; suede or antelope for high occasions. Have plenty of white gloves, washable too, for nothing dresses one up like fresh, white gloves. White cotton fabric gloves for summer, washable kid in winter.

A bride needs a good coat. A coat that may be worn over dresses or a suit—in fact, over everything but evening clothes—is recommended. This should not be a sports coat, but one cut without fussy detail, and it should go with the basic colors of her wardrobe. A fur scarf or stole has many uses; it may be worn in the day or evening, and takes care of the problem of an evening wrap except in bitter weather. A satin stole, made of the full width of the fabric, two and a half yards long, makes a fairly opulent evening wrap and takes up little room at home or traveling, for it folds flat. In fact, a good-looking stole, provided it is wide enough, makes a very practical auxiliary wrap. Of heavy tweed, rough wool, or jersey, it may be worn with suits or sports clothes; of more elegant fabric, with dresses for day or cocktail time.

Sports clothes belong in the wardrobe of a bride whose life calls for them. If she lives in the city, she may not need them except at vacation time. But active sportswomen know their needs better than anyone else. Frocks for golf or tennis, riding or skiing clothes, slacks, shorts, play clothes, all must suit individual needs.

Trousseau time is the time to begin this new habit of buying clothes that will be suitable and useful as long as they hold together.

The trousseau isn't for show. It isn't got together to vie with another girl—to outdo her. It is a bride's outward personality sincerely expressed.

THE HOUSEHOLD TROUSSEAU

The hope chest may have gone the way of the stage coach, but what was stored in it is today a practical part of the trousseau, equally important with the bride's personal trousseau. Eventually more so. Though hope-chest treasures now are labeled with words strange to brides of yesteryear, telling of fabrics and colors they never heard of, the linens for dining room and kitchen, bedroom and bath, still bear titles known to generations of housewives. Nothing stands higher in the eyes of the neophyte lady of the house. No bride is superior to the magnetic power of fresh clean linen. The spirit of the hope chest still lives in the new home.

When it comes to planning the household trousseau, even a bride with her head in the clouds should have her feet solidly on the ground. If she is serious and down-to-earth in her approach to her choice of linens, she may make a mistake through lack of knowledge but not through emotional choosing. Sentiment rarely leads her astray. Each item of her household trousseau is bought for a purpose, and even a newly engaged young woman has heard something about the problems and hazards of fine laundering.

Linens, like her clothes and the furniture of her home, reflect what is going on in the world. They bear the signs of the times. Therefore, today's bridal linens, though traditional in their purpose, differ considerably from those of a trousseau of even twenty-five years ago. The life of a bride today is more streamlined, her linens along with everything else. Reminders of the past—laces, appliqués, Victorian embroideries, and other fancies—are still a delight to own; but simplicity and utility, tied in with quality, rule the basic scheme of selection.

A young woman setting out to choose linens today should buy the best known brands in bed and bath linens, as well as the linens for table and kitchen, from a store with a reputation for substantial and honest dealing. The things to stick closest to are those classic in quality and design.

Undoubtedly a bride's table linen is most likely to engage her first interest and attention, because it shows off her new silver and china. It is in this setting that she wishes her friends to assess her abilities as hostess when they see her presiding at her table. But there are other departments equally important. In purchases here she learns in practical terms that she is not buying for herself only, but for somebody else as well. In selecting bath towels, for instance, she must consider her husband, who will not be satisfied with small, thin bath towels. A man's bath towel should be at least 46 by 24 inches, and the heavier they are, the longer they will last and the pleasanter they are to use.

A husband may not know a great deal about the material his bed linens are made of, but he will know without a doubt if sheets are too short or too narrow. He may not know why his bed is not comfortable, but he will certainly be aware of discomfort. Never buy sheets that are too short or too narrow, nor pillow cases that are too tight. The pillows themselves ideally should be filled with the best quality of feathers or down, free of odor.

A bride of today should consider the fitted bottom sheet if her training has not taught her to turn a square, hospital-shaped corner which insures a wrinkle-free bed.

A beginner's list which a bride may amplify should include:

8 sheets and 8 pillow cases for each bed, single or double
4 bath towels per person
4 extra bath towels for guests
4 Turkish hand towels and 4 washcloths per person
1 dozen linen guest towels between hand and fingertip size
5 different sets of plastic mats with colorful napkins for daily use
2 informal woven doily sets of practical, sturdy materials that may be sent to any laundry without fear. One of these sets should be for eight people, the other for four.
1 handsome doily set for eight or twelve, which will be a beautiful background for silver and china

In this list we have not included blankets, comfortables, or blanket covers because they are favorite wedding presents from members of the families. To make the record complete, brides in the so-called temperate zones will need a pair of blankets for each bed and at least two blanket covers per bed. A comfortable of down, wool, or dacron for each bed is a practical and beautiful necessity.

When it is possible, plan bathroom colors before buying towels, and then adjust colors of towels or monograms to the plan without matching colors slavishly. Several pastels, or two tones of a single color, may work out very happily in the same bathroom. For guest towels use the same or harmonizing colors of the big bath towels. These should be of fine linen huck, which is both good-looking and long-wearing when it gets the treatment it deserves.

There should be plenty of practical, inexpensive sets of plastic or woven table mats for day-by-day use. For formal meals have two or three doily sets, tailored or with a modest appliqué in a favorite color. And every household needs one or two sets of fine table linen for festive entertaining such as birthdays and anniversaries. These are kept for high occasions and should go with the period of dining-room furniture, china, silver, and glass. White or pastel organdy cloths with full dinner-size napkins fall into this class. The more formal cloth requires perfect fit; this means the same drop all around, not less than ten inches. Napkins for dining should be twenty-two inches square, or they may be 16-by-24-inch oblongs for the formal table. They are pretty generally known as "lapkins," and though the word may be coy, they are handsome stand-ins for the conventional, square napkins. If rayon is chosen, and very beautiful rayon damask is being made, select it in ivory or pastels; if linen, preferably white or ivory.

A colorful buffet cloth of fine quality, with at least twelve large napkins, is a handsome addition to the linen trousseau, if the budget is generous. And it is useful to have matching or contrasting bridge cloths to go with the buffet cloth, since bridge tables are most often used for this sort of popular informal dining. In fact, little tablecloths for teas or informal bites taken at the bridge table must not be forgotten. To go with these small cloths, it is a good idea to buy extra napkins for friends who drop in, but it is worth remembering that if napkins are too small they fall off laps persistently and may be mistaken for handkerchiefs and disappear in someone's coat pocket.

We approve the old-time housewife who respected her sturdy kitchen linens by giving them dignity with a simple quickly done cross-stitch initial, yet we know our modern girl too well to expect her to go that far. It is a fact that a kitchen with properly cared for towels neatly dressed up with small initials is a pleasant sight, but the modern bride can add a bright, crisp touch to her kitchen decor in a dozen ways. In fact, the imagination displayed by modern designers and the variety of color, fabric, and pattern in linen departments give a girl establishing a new home great scope in her planning of the style and color schemes to be used in bath and bedroom. Shops everywhere cooperate in many instances by keeping a file of monograms and colors chosen for trousseau linens so that replacements or additions may be ordered with a minimum of trouble, and these records are valuable for intra-family giving.

The dishwasher, to be sure, is a valued accessory in the kitchen of today's bride; but good towels, to give china and especially glasses and silver a final loving polish, are necessary. They are good-looking to boot. The old admonishment that such towels should be lint-free and absorbent still holds good.

It is a wise forethought to keep a memorandum of the size of the dining table with its extensions and the dimensions of mattresses. Simple but valuable advice for an extended life expectancy is to give all linens a chance to rest by rotating them. When they are washed, freshly laundered things should be put at the bottom of the pile. An identification mark should be on every piece. This makes for permanency and often calls errant linens home to roost if they go to a large laundry.

She sends out the invitations and announcements

Making up the lists of invitations and announcements is a joint collaboration between the bride and her mother and the groom and his mother. The final list is an amalgamation of both lists, carefully checked to eliminate duplicates.

If the families of the engaged couple are close friends, they are likely to have approximately the same lists. This will be augmented by additions of relatives and friends from other cities, to be supplied by both families. Should the groom's family live in another city, more invitations may be sent than if both families lived near each other, since many of his acquaintances naturally will not be those of his bride.

When a large church wedding is to be followed by a reception, the groom's mother will furnish a list of those to be invited to the reception.

Invitations to a large church wedding are always sent to the entire lists of both families, no matter how large they may be, or whether or not they can be present. People in mourning are included.

Invitations to a formal wedding should be formal, that is, they should be engraved and sent by mail. Except in emergency, guests should never be invited by telephone or telegraph. If the public is not to be admitted to the church, a door card is usually enclosed with the invitation.

A formal invitation requires two envelopes. The inner envelope, in which the invitation and reception card are enclosed, is not sealed. It bears only the name of the person to whom it is addressed. This envelope is placed in the outer one, with the name facing the back in order that it may be read at once when it is removed. The outer envelope is sealed and bears the complete name and address of the person to whom it is sent. It is not in good taste to send invitations unsealed at a lesser rate of postage.

Every adult member of a family should receive an individual invitation, with one exception. A husband and wife are addressed together. If children twelve or under are to be invited, their names without surname may be written below their parents' on the inside envelope, as "Charles, Mary, Christine."

Invitations to a wedding in church do not require an answer, and R.S.V.P. is never engraved upon them.

Invitations should be mailed a month or three weeks before the wedding, and ordered from the engraver from six weeks to two months before they are to go into the mail.

If guests to be invited are few, the invitations may be personal notes written by the bride and her mother. The invitation always goes in the name of the bride's mother. Sending it by telegraph or telephone is a modern expedient, admissible where time is short.

The written invitation for a small wedding, the engraved invitation for a large one, are worthwhile observances of traditional form for an important occasion.

More guests are usually invited to the wedding ceremony than to the reception. When this is the case, a reception card should be enclosed with the invitation for those who are invited to attend the reception.

If a bride decides on a ceremony with guests restricted to members of the immediate families and a large reception to follow, those invited to the reception should receive an invitation in form and size exactly like the wedding invitation.

An invitation to a church wedding requires no reply. An invitation to the reception should be answered immediately and in writing. The response follows the form of the invitation, written in the third person.

Announcements of the wedding are sent to persons who do not receive invitations. These go out immediately after a small wedding at home or a private ceremony which is limited to relatives and close personal friends. Such general announcements go to the entire lists of both families and often to business acquaintances. The style of engraving should be the same as selected for the wedding invitations.

The envelopes should be addressed and ready for mailing before the ceremony, and posted immediately after the wedding.

She chooses her wedding attendants

As in many other aspects of the wedding, the attendants are a modern expression of ancient customs. The bride has her maid, or matron, of honor and bridesmaids; the groom his best man and ushers. How many should make up today's wedding party is a matter of choice with the bride and groom, the same as the size and elaboration of the wedding.

Many bridesmaids belong to the formal wedding party, and there are more of them in bridal parties today than a few years ago.

If a bride is married in a street dress or going-away costume, she will have an honor attendant, but no bridesmaids.

A large wedding can scarcely have too many ushers. While bridesmaids are there to be seen, ushers have duties. There should always be several of them; at a very large wedding there may be a dozen. A church wedding of size demands a number, a house wedding none. A garden wedding may find half a dozen useful.

She plans pre-wedding dinners and parties

Entertainments previous to the wedding day for the wedding party and close friends of the bride and groom are usually three: a bridal luncheon or tea given by the bride for her honor attendant and bridesmaids, a bridal dinner, and the groom's bachelor dinner.

The luncheon or tea for the bride's attendants is a "must". It is often given on the day a bride has a final fitting of her wedding gown, and a final try-on of her bridal headdress. This is also a good day for her bridesmaids to have their final fittings. It is also a practical time for formal bridal photographs.

This luncheon gives the bride an opportunity to show her trousseau and to present her gifts to her wedding attendants.

More often than not the bridal dinner is given by an aunt or grandmother of the bride a few days before the wedding. Or it may be given by the parents of the groom, especially if they live in the same city. To this party all members of the bridal party, parents of bride and groom, and the officiating clergyman and his wife should be invited. Since everyone who is to take part in the ceremony is on hand, this is a perfect time to rehearse the wedding, before or after the dinner. This dinner is sometimes the evening before the wedding; yet it is better, if possible, for this evening to be left free for a bride to spend it with her family. Old-fashioned, perhaps, but it makes as much sense as sentiment.

At the dinner the bride and groom are seated side by side, the bride on the groom's right. The honor attendant sits to the left of the groom, the best man to the right of the bride. Parents of bride and groom are placed opposite the bridal party, and the protocol of their seating depends upon who is giving the dinner.

A proper pattern is as follows: mother of groom, bride's father to her left, clergyman to her right, mother of bride to right of clergyman, wife of clergyman to left of bride's father. Bridesmaids and ushers alternate at the sides of the table.

This meal, in tune with modern entertaining, is most often a buffet supper, following a late-afternoon rehearsal. And very often a busy modern clergyman may excuse himself for rehearsal or dinner.

She buys a present for the groom

A bride's present to her groom will also be one of enduring quality. If he is still wearing his schoolboy watch, her problem is simple, for a fine timepiece is at the top of the list of what men want. A watch is more than a simple timepiece; it may be a definite part of the equipment for his profession or favorite sport. So, we have chronographs, timers specifically for doctors or for sports cars or for boat or horse racing. A man who already has a sturdy water-resistant and shock-proof watch for daytime may like a wafer-thin dress watch for evening and formal wear. Cufflinks for day or evening, and some of them with shirt studs added, may double for both, and are favored gifts to the groom. If a man wears a pocket watch, a chain for it with a pencil or knife for the other end is an apt present, as is a plain gold or jeweled tie clasp. Whenever possible these presents are initialed or monogrammed, and, however small, engraved with the wedding date even if it must go on the back.

She finds tokens for her attendants

Gifts to bridesmaids and ushers range over a broad field from modest remembrances to expensive presents. A bride frequently picks for her honor attendant and bridesmaids such things as a crystal perfume bottle for dressing-table use, or small silver ones to carry in a purse, lipstick cases, compacts for solid or loose powder, a silver-or gold-mounted comb, traveling clocks, a bracelet with an inscribed charm, or a bill clip, earrings, or gold bobby pins.

GIFTS OF ATTENDANTS TO BRIDE AND GROOM

Bridesmaids usually band together for a gift to the bride, and this gift may be a personal present such as the traditional silver comb, brush, and mirror to deck a dressing table, or a velvet-lined silver jewel box. Bridesmaids often choose instead a present of the distinctly wedding-gift type. Of these a silver water pitcher, a card tray—which may be used for cards or hors d'oeuvres—or a sandwich tray with scrolled handles, to give some favorite instances. These gifts to the bride, especially personal ones, will be monogrammed. For some esoteric reason bridesmaids seldom go in for the facsimile signatures on a gleaming silver surface often presented by the men of the bridal party.

She selects her gift patterns

A wedding present is a traditional gift with a unique purpose. It is a permanent means of conveying the affection and good wishes of family and friends of the bride and groom. As this gift helps to form the nucleus of a new home, it should be chosen with very special thought. It must combine those features of good taste and quality that will endure with the years.

Choosing a wedding gift is never the bugaboo sometimes conjured up by a stalled or apprehensive mind. Though it may at first glance seem a problem, it usually turns out to be a quite simple selection. The reason is not hard to see. In one of half a dozen ways, a bride herself sets the pattern for most of the gifts she will receive, and one and all of the friends and relatives of bride and groom choose presents that dovetail with that pattern. In this realistic and eminently practical age a bride does not hesitate to let it be known what designs in silver, in china, in glassware, and even in linens she has selected for her house, and people in the throes of wedding-present shopping welcome the hint.

In every city there is sure to be one shop or more with a record of the patterns of silver and china a bride has selected. Begun as an unofficial expedient to help a wedding guest augment the basic material a bride has chosen herself, it has developed into the well-recognized and notably helpful bride's register. Undeniably, this facilitates the selection of wedding gifts, saving time and effort for busy people. But for everyone it adds the assurance that the gift will be welcomed wholeheartedly—a comfortable feeling, especially if there is not intimate acquaintance with the bride and her tastes.

Professional guidance in setting the pattern for her silver, china, glassware, and linens is based upon where a bride is to set up housekeeping, and whether her furnishings will be contemporary or traditional. Often her selections will depend on the home she hopes to have some day, with perhaps a small apartment for her immediate post-honeymoon home. As generations of brides before her have done, she will choose first of all the pattern of her silver, for it is basic and permanent. It will influence her choice of china and glassware, and of the linen that will go with all three. At the same time her taste in monograms, her color preferences for linens, and in many instances the color schemes she will have in her home may be listed. All this data is of real value in deciding upon a gift.

By old convention, flat silver is given by the family of the bride, and hollow ware, such as vegetable and dessert dishes and meat platters, by the groom's family. But this need not stop a generous donor who wishes to do handsomely by a young pair. A service for after-dinner coffee or, for that matter, a combination tea and coffee service, or beautiful trays to set them on, all are gifts as cherished by today's brides as by their grandmothers before them. But brides also like small pieces of useful silver, easily portable, which may serve in a temporary home if her husband still has to do his military service. Such small things as a sugar bowl and creamer, numberless leaf-shaped dishes which may be used for nuts, candy, or even ashes, are both handsome and practical, and well within a minimal figure set for a wedding present.

To the individualist who would like to register his own taste and influence in the new home, small useful antiquities that add grace to a dinner table or living room are appealing. Antique ladles in various sizes, old stuffing spoons or a pair of servers, marrow spoons or cheese scoops, to be used as modern cocktail stirrers, are a few things quickly available to shoppers. A silver skewer, once used to hold a lordly joint in shape, makes a handsome accessory for a desk as an efficient paper cutter. Small silver patch boxes or snuffboxes for vitamin or aspirin tablets, and larger boxes for cigarettes or candy or tea, are among well-liked elegancies many brides will welcome. No one wastes time or money if he considers a fine piece of old crystal or china, dessert or service plates, or small pieces such as a covered sauce boat—large enough to use as a soup tureen for two—or a footed stand for cake or fruit. Any of these and many others from the porcelain factories of Worcester, Spode, or Wedgwood, to name several, are engaging accessories. Antique silver and porcelain are accompanied by a small card upon which is noted origin, date, and maker when possible, all of which add interest and cachet to the gift.

It is well to remember that young people seldom have unlimited money to spend on themselves, that they are building a future, and that it may be years before they are able to buy for themselves many things that would fit beautifully into their household, things they would love to own. Those who are about to begin housekeeping at once have in all probability planned, and perhaps bought, most of the substantial and basic furnishings for their first home. Whatever will add beauty to it, or augment their silver, china, glass, or other appurtenances of graceful living, will be more than a gift.

She keeps a record of her gifts

It would be unforgivable for any bride to receive gifts for her engagement and wedding without preparing herself to send out thank-you notes at a later date, not missing a single donor and being able to remember what each has given her. This is not only a duty but a pleasure, since in years to come it is rewarding to be reminded of your friends and relatives as you live in a home beautified by their gifts.

Here is the best system to guard against any errors or forgotten items. The bride purchases an alphabetized notebook, and a set of small, numbered, gummed stickers, with the numbers running from one to two hundred (or more if a great many gifts are expected). As each gift is received, she makes a note in her book of the donor and his or her address. Next to this she puts a capsule description of the gift—"silver pitcher with initials and dolphin handle"—which will serve her well later on in writing her thank-you notes. Then, as each gift is received, she affixes one of the stickers to it as inconspicuously as possible, and records the same number next to the name of the donor in her book. This system of checks and double checks guarantees that no one will be forgotten, and the bride shows by her care in remembering the nature of every gift that she truly appreciates each generous remembrance.

On page 202, there is space for your own gift recording. This may be utilized in the manner described, and may also serve as a permanent record of your wedding acquisitions.

She symbolizes love in bloom with flowers

Whatever the time of year there are flowers to add their beauty to the scene, and, like the bridesmaids, they build up the bride, spotlighting her at all times. They are present to add grace to the scene, not to overpower it and draw attention to themselves. Whether many or few, they need to be selected and arranged so that they are never obtrusive: fragrantly elegant rather than flamboyant. Yet next to the bride's gown and veil, her bouquet is the most important part of her costume. It emphasizes and complements her gown and definitely sounds the floral keynote for the entire bridal party.

Flowers are only too welcome. They pose the danger of superfluity: too many flowers, too haphazardly selected, and too carelessly assembled. They must never be incidental nor accidental on the bridal agenda. The minute a bride-elect has chosen her wedding gown, whether it is satin and rosepoint in the grand manner or a floor-length dress of organdy, her first stop ought to be the florist. And with her she should have a sample of her wedding gown, to show its exact tone of white, and a picture of it if possible. A bridal bouquet must be in the mood and fashion of the bridal gown; it should harmonize with it and with the bride's height and type. If she is a neat five feet, and has chosen a bouffant gown, a sheaf of calla lilies is not for her. Unless her bridal gown is a period piece, she should avoid the compact, old-fashioned colonial bouquet, hard and tight as a small head of winter cabbage. Her florist has far, far better ideas in store for her.

ALL FLOWERS ARE BRIDAL FLOWERS

Best news for the bride is that all flowers are bridal flowers. If she has a favorite flower, it can be used, no matter how perishable—the ox-eyed daisy, or fragrant but quickly drooping flowers such as the hyacinth, white lilac, narcissus, tulip, and all the fragile spring flowers. By a brand-new technique, which is a trade secret, her florist seals each cut stem of every flower, imprisoning at the same time enough water to keep them triumphantly fresh throughout the wedding ceremony and reception.

BRIDAL BOUQUETS

Florists were never so imaginative in their approach to new design, nor so skillful in choosing and manipulating flowers to go with a new and beautiful bridal fashion or fabric. Happily, a bride always has a great variety of new floral designs to select from, unlike her mother and grandmother whose bridal finery was invariably overpowered by an immense shower bouquet dripping with baby ribbon—and unvarying *fin de siècle* flower fashion that lasted well into the twenties. But the shower bouquet, basically a sound idea, has not been jettisoned by florists. Far from it. Today's bride carries the cascade, an airy flower confection in which such small blossoms as white violets, florets of freesia, stock, or delphinium fall from an arrangement of the same flowers, or perhaps from a cluster of baby orchids, roses, or eucharis lilies. There is another invention, identified by a newly coined word, "basquet," a logical combination of "basket" and "bouquet" and pronounced *baskay*. It is a basket entirely made of flowers, with blossoms spilling over its sides, and carried by a ribbon-bound handle. Another beguiling version, deriving though remotely from the shower bouquet, employs splendid gardenias, duchess roses, camellias, or any flower a bride loves, to make a burst of flowers from which pendant sections like floating garlands are suspended so that they hang gracefully at no matter what angle the bouquet is held.

Old-fashioned bouquets are still a love of today's brides. But instead of the row upon row of tightly massed flowers, they are smaller, lightly gathered arrangements, with no dangling ribbons, no stiff frill of lace paper, though there is often a frill of flower petals. An unusual and winning idea is one in which carnations are set closely together in the shape of a ball, with ribbons to carry it by, and looks like an old-fashioned reticule. Both of these are particularly effective carried by brides in bouffant, summery dresses.

Winter brides often carry muffs of flowers, frilly tulle or lace, velvet or satin, tufted with small blooms, or bedecked with gardenias, camellias, or orchids. These bewitching trifles must not be used in summer, no matter how sheer the material.

Sometimes a fine-lace fan with ivory or mother-of-pearl sticks is a family possession and a bride may wish to carry it instead of a bouquet. Florists have many ideas to make it a graceful and easily managed accessory. For instance, a bracelet of white flowers, with a delicate shower of blossom-studded ribbons—florets of stock, white violets, or the petals of white carnations shaped into minikin blossoms to wear with the fan partly open. Or a small cluster of flowers fastened to the handle with a tiny spray of flowerets, the fan to be carried open. Fans are a delightful accessory when deftly handled by both florist and bride; worth the effort when the fan is beautiful.

A prayer book to be used in the marriage service is the choice of many brides who wish to keep it as a memento of The Day. It is possible to buy beautifully bound and decorated prayer books, but if you wish to use one not bound in white, it may be easily given a slip cover of white satin or brocade, a simple chore for even a butter-fingered bride. It may bear a single fine orchid, a gardenia, or camellia, or eucharis lilies with stephanotis or lilies of the valley. Or the book may have a flower-decked ribbon marker placed at the service from which the clergyman may read.

Bouquets today are symmetrical, so that they are lovely from any angle, as pretty from both sides of the aisle as they are beautiful in front. They are invariably made so that they may be held gracefully, in order that the flowers as well as the bridal gown be seen to advantage. One of the best is a small wand which may be held lightly but securely. Greens are used carefully, just a sprinkling of fine baby ivy, pale green and white caladium leaves, or perhaps young pandanus veitchii, which can be folded into ribbonlike loops. At times a bride may like to have the color of her attendants' gowns reflected in her own bouquet. For this pale pink sweetheart roses, faintly blue delphinium, or even the deeper blue of cornflowers are set delicately and sparingly behind the white flowers of a bouquet.

BRIDAL HEADDRESSES

Bridal headdresses to be worn with a veil are particularly appealing when beautifully executed. A bandeau, a wreath, or a low tiara very slightly raised in the center, and with flowers radiating from the sides, should be made of some of the flowers from a bride's bouquet, never of lilies of the valley or orange blossoms unless they are repeated in her bouquet. It is an engaging fashion for very young brides. Head-dresses are made with tiny loops so that they may be securely fastened with fine hairpins or bobby pins.

BOUQUETS FOR BRIDAL ATTENDANTS

In design, and size and mood, the bouquets of bridal attendants second the bride's own. While it is true that in an all-white wedding a bride and her maids carry the same flowers, with their bouquets perhaps of different shape, a bride is starred more effectively if her maids carry colored posies, brilliant or pastel. If a bride carries white daisies, her attendants will have painted daisies or African daisies. Occasionally it is possible to match exactly the color of the bridesmaids' dresses in the flowers they carry; this is an interesting floral stunt, for the different values of flower petals and fabrics can be very effective. But the colors must be carefully matched from swatches of the material.

A flower girl seldom scatters rose petals in the path of today's bride, but in every other way one is as blossomy as her title suggests. She may carry a basket of baby flowers or a miniature nosegay, or a diminutive cage fashioned of flowers with flowers within. She may wear a wreath or crown of flowers, or a cluster of flowerets fastened to a barrette to hold her curls in a center or side parting. If her hair is smooth and straight, she may have an Alice in Wonderland flower-covered round comb or bicycle clip. Sometimes hoops wrapped with ribbon and adorned with minute flowers are designed for tots, but children are at their best when their props are uncomplicated and easy to cope with.

FLOWERS AT THE RECEPTION

The trend is toward a natural treatment of flowery decor; to elegance instead of elaboration, whether for a reception at home or in a suite of parlors in a hotel or club. There should be a background for the receiving line. At times the key point in a room is before a great sheet of mirror, and when this is the case it is screened with delicate greenery, such as the exquisite old-time favorite, smilax, to serve as a background for festoons of flowers. To feature the receiving line further, huge arrangements of flowers at each side dramatize the bridal group, and these two important groups of flowers may be used

to mark the setting for the receiving party wherever the reception takes place. When the reception is at home, enough flowers should be used to create a gala atmosphere, but no more.

She mulls over menus

A wedding reception is a joyous occasion, though not without solemnity, and the preparations should be intelligently and carefully planned by the hostess, whether it is held at a home, hotel, restaurant, or club.

It has been said, and often with good cause, that the wedding comes as a relief to the harried young couple, who try to keep up with the luncheons, cocktail parties, and dinner invitations their friends and families shower on them before the wedding. Therefore for many brides a "little home wedding reception" also comes as a great relief, in addition to being a memorable evening spent in the company of a few friends and relatives; besides, there is the care and attention that a hostess can give even today with limited or no domestic help.

Perfection with ease and comfort should be the goal for this propitious occasion, and this can be accomplished only if the planner begins with a full understanding of the limitations as well as the capabilities of a catering or family staff.

For a successful home wedding reception set for four thirty or five, where preparations will be made in the family kitchen with or without a caterer's help, we recommend a cold, simple menu with the possible exception of the soup and of course the tea and coffee, first because of the weather, since it is more likely to be summer, and second because it is so much easier to prepare. The menu follows:

Champagne or
Wine Punch

Supreme of Fresh Fruits
with Melon Balls
(flavored with Bristol Cream Sherry)

❋

Strained Consommé in Cups
with Tapioca Pearls

❋

Fancy Assorted Tea Sandwiches
(cut in fours)

❋

Wedding-Form Ice Creams
Petits Fours
Wedding Cake

❋

Tea or Coffee

This menu can be amplified by adding a salad of chicken or lobster or crab ravigote, or even something hot, i.e., chicken à la king, or curried sweetbreads with Madras rice, served from a chafing dish. Bear in mind that any "addition" should be easy to eat, preferably with a fork. (No "cut with knife first and then eat" inconvenience.) If no caterer is engaged, it is a wise policy to have a waiter or two on hand, one to serve and help guests with the food and the other for mixing and serving drinks.

We would like to stress: stay away from completely hot menus; dishes that have to be kept at a special temperature, served at a specific time, or made while guests are present; dishes that cannot be easily eaten with hand or fork; and dishes that have not been tried before, perhaps terribly unusual ones, which three quarters of the guests will not recognize and probably will not like.

It is recommended to serve foods that have been tried and that appeal to most people, perhaps adding an original touch such as shape, size, or color. A point to bring out at this time is to be aware of color schemes. In planning each course try to imagine how it will blend with other items: flowers, table linen, decorations, and other foods.

Of course, everything should be set up before the arrival of the guests: table dishes, silverware, glasses, napkins, etc. And be sure these are easily accessible. The room or rooms should have a minimum of furniture, with occasional comfortable chairs, small tables, and possibly folding chairs which can be brought out only if needed.

If this is a first "try," keep the guest list down to a maximum of fifty to avoid any feeling of pretentiousness, and keep the expense within the limits of the budget; the bride will then gain the best results of cordiality, ease, comfort, and warmth among her friends and guests. In other words, "Don't overdo it."

The wedding cake should be baked, if not at home, by a reliable bakery. Since it plays such an important part in the wedding celebration, it should be handsomely decorated, preferably with royal or fudge icing instead of whipped cream, which sours easily.

The small wedding at home, in conclusion, should be simple but faultless, with a feeling not of effort but of complete ease and serenity.

If there is to be an early-morning wedding (ten A.M.), a typically "breakfast" menu at about noon should be served; and this should include, instead of browned country sausage or the usual egg dishes, eggs Benedictine, or a small croustade filled with freshly made scrambled eggs with chicken livers and *fine herbes* for instance. A fruit appetizer to start and a fancy dessert will round out a lovely menu.

A luncheon following a high-noon wedding (twelve thirty P.M.) would be better served in a private suite at a hotel, or at a town or country club, and should include seasonal food dishes. For instance:

WEDDING LUNCHEON

*Champagne
passed on
trays*

Suprême of Oranges
and Pink Grapefruit
Served in Champagne Glasses
Decorated with Sugar Lovebirds
Tied with White Satin Bows

✺

Consommé Bellevue
with Whipped Cream
in Cups
Small Heart-Shaped Cheese Sticks

✺

Squab Chicken Souvaroff
Boned and Stuffed with Wild Rice
Served in Round Silver Covers
Nest of Potatoes with
Smothered New Peas
Broccoli Mimosa

✺

Heart-Shaped Raspberry and Vanilla Ice Creams
on Ice Socle
Hot Brandied Strawberries Flambée
in Chafing Dish
Flower-Shaped Petits Fours
Wedding Cake

✻

Demi-Tasse with Fresh Mint

A wedding dinner at six or later should be imaginative and of elegant simplicity but not too elaborate—in other words, a menu for a bridal party not intent on cutting costs and definitely held at a hotel or a large restaurant with banquet facilities. Such as this:

WEDDING DINNER

Mailly Rose Champagne
Sherry, Cocktails,
and Highballs
only on request

An Elaborate Smorgasbord, including:
Sides of Nova Scotia Salmon
Stuffed Squabs with Chicken Salami
Anchovies, Stuffed Olives
Small Gefüllte Fish
Whole Turkeys Découpé et Remonté
Whole Ducklings Découpé et Remonté
Ox Tongue en Bellevue, Stuffed Celery
with Chicken Livers and Anchovy
(To be served from large buffet table
with two elevations.

Waiters serving buffet to be dressed in chef's uniforms.)
Two Large Sculptured Lighted Ice Socles

❈

An Excellent Assortment of
Hot and Cold Appetizers, including:
Liver Puffs, Hot Barquettes,
Knishes, Chopped Steak Balls, etc.,
passed on trays by waiters
and served from chafing dishes
Suprême of Fresh Fruit Princess
Decorated with Blue Sugar Lovebirds
Served on Ice in Silver Cups
tied with Pale Blue Ribbon
on Gold Doily

❈

*Château Haut
Brion Blanc 1952
Magnums*

Brook Trout à la Lucullus
(boned and stuffed with
Purée of Salmon) en Gelée
Sauce Verte
Cucumbers Vernon

❈

Petite Marmite Henri IV
(with Diced Vegetables and White Meat of Chicken)
French Croutons

❈

Hearts of Celery   Ripe and Green Olives
Salted Nuts

❈

Besserat de
Bellefon
1949 Jeroboams

Jumbo Squab Royale Farcie
with Special Wild-Rice Dressing
Baby Belgian Carrots
Asparagus Tips Polonaise
Old-Fashioned Spiced Peaches

❋

Winter Salad à la Joan Diane
with Avocado Pear, Endive, and Cherry Tomatoes
Oil and Lemon Dressing

❋

Lovebirds of Praline Ice Cream
Rolled in Fresh Pink-Colored Coconut
and Served on Decorated Ice Socle
Petits Fours   Sugar Fruits
Wedding Cake

❋

Godet Cuvé '51
Marsan Armagnac Private Reserve
Vieille Curé
French Green-Mint Frappé

Demi-Tasse
Served with Fresh Mint
and Cinnamon Stick

A buffet served at any time from six to nine P.M. seems to be preferred by many brides because of its informality. Without wishing to
disillusion anybody, it can also be, quite unhappily, most confusing
and costly unless it is well planned and superbly executed, with as

many waiters as for a seated dinner. It must be remembered that a lavish "choice" is the first requirement of a buffet, so a certain amount of waste is unavoidable and a resultant higher cost is inescapable to really make a buffet successful. Here is a sample menu:

---⊰ WEDDING BUFFET ⊱---

Sherry, Mailly Pink and
White Champagne

Finger Toasts of Smoked Salmon,
Sturgeon and Waldorf Pâté
Stuffed Giant Green and Black Olives
Stuffed Celery and Sardines
Arranged on Zodiac Platters
with Special Presentation
Hot Bouchées of Crabmeat
Hot Fried Shrimps
(very hot, cooked fresh)
Clams Casino, Oysters Rockefeller
Served from Large Warmers
Hot Double Tomato Madrilène
with Florida Pearls
in Cups
Lucullus Crusts

✳

hot   Italian Ravioli
in Chafing Dish
Breaded Semiboned Half Baby Chickens
à la Governor Olivier
Lobster Américaine
Buttered Pilaff Rice
in Chafing Dish

Small Bouchées of Chicken à la King
(well-flavored sauce)
Hot French White Beans

❋

cold
Celery à la Grecque
Cold Stuffed Roast Turkeys
(découpé, cut on the bone, French style)
Prime Ribs of Beef
(découpé et remonté)
Ox Tongues en Bellevue
Stringbeans and Tomatoes Vinaigrette
Potato Salad Mayonnaise
Baby Artichokes and Hearts of Palm
White Leaves of Lettuce Salad
Vinaigrette Dressing
Cold Kennebec Salmon
(large size, completely boned and stuffed,
with special decoration)
Long Buttered French Bread
(Served warm at each table, in napkins)
Plain Buttered Rolls

❋

Very large, attractive Ice Pieces
with Compotiers of Fresh Fruits and Melons
Macédoine of Fresh Fruits
with plenty of Strawberries, Berries, and Melons
(on ice, in large punch bowls,
with special presentation)
Large Pineapples, on Ice
Filled with Coconut-Pineapple Ice Cream
To Be Served with Fresh Fruit
Served on Ice, in Large Punch Bowls
Large Babas au Rhum

Large French Strawberry, Blueberry,
Apple, and Pear Tarts
Large French Chocolate Cakes
Small Dainty Danish Pastries
Wedding Cake

❋

Coffee   Tea
Cold Milk

She puts punch into the proceedings

The wedding drink is, of course, champagne, and everyone present will want to drink it in the traditional toast to the happy couple. The father of the bride, faced with the horrendous task of cornering enough champagne for his guests, does well to provide imported bubbly for the direct members of the bridal party, since this is strictly a once-in-a-lifetime occasion. But if the guests at the reception are there in force, and prices on imported champagne being what they are, he is advised to serve them domestic champagne, of which there are a number of excellent varieties. Drinks of all kinds should be made available after the first flowing of the champagne, and to keep the moment festive on the liquid menu, several bowls of punch are recommended. Confirmed nondrinkers will probably steer a path toward Cokes or Seven-Up, but the two bowls of punch can also be helpful in the light of the guests' choices by being graded as to strength.

First, let us look at the milder punch.

A fine punch may be made with light Rhine wine. Three quarts of Rhine wine, one quart of chilled soda water, three jiggers of brandy, three jiggers of maraschino, one cup of strong tea, and one half pound of sugar are the ingredients. Combine all of the makings in a punch bowl surrounded by a bed of ice, but do not put the ice directly into the drink. Decorate with colorful pieces of fruit, a few sprigs of mint if available, and serve thoroughly chilled. This recipe will provide

from twenty-five to thirty cups of wonderfully fresh-tasting punch which does not contain too much of a knockout.

A very handsome punch can be made with these ingredients: juice of two lemons and two oranges, one wineglass of brandy, one wineglass of curaçao, one glass of raspberry syrup, two bottles of sparkling Burgundy, and one quart of soda water. Mix all of these ingredients except the sparkling Burgundy and the soda water in the punch bowl, and put in enough ice to chill well. The Burgundy and soda are added last, pouring carefully and stirring lightly, but not enough to dissipate too many of their sparkling bubbles. The recipe will serve eighteen, and looks extremely inviting with its deep red color. But once again, the punch, although delicious, has a limited kick, and will appeal to the careful drinkers.

On the stronger side, there are many variations, and practically every liquor store will have little booklets, especially those prepared by the wine and rum dispensers, which suggest how to make a one-two punch. One of the simplest is made with good old applejack. Take two quarts of applejack, four jiggers of grenadine, one pint of orange juice. Pour into a punch bowl over a block of ice. Just before serving add two quarts of ginger ale. Decorate with fruit, as desired. Add cider to stretch the drink and weaken its kick, if desired. This recipe will serve from twenty-five to thirty guests.

Boston Fish House Punch is one of the glories of Colonial times which has come down to us for special occasions. Here is a recipe to make fifty guests properly joyous: First put into a sizable punch bowl one tumbler of melted sugar, one tumbler of lime juice or one and one half tumblers of lemon juice, and then mix all of these ingredients very thoroughly until the sugar is completely dissolved into the liquids. Now add one and one half bottles of Jamaica rum, one bottle of brandy, one tumbler of peach brandy, and three quarts of champagne. Chill with large chunks of ice.

There are a number of good champagne recipes that fit beautifully into the occasion. Here is a regal combination: For every bottle of champagne, add one wineglass of maraschino, one wineglass of yellow chartreuse, one full glass of brandy, and one pint of sparkling water. One half lemon and one whole orange, both sliced, are added. You can figure on from six to eight glasses per bottle.

A sight for thirsty guests in this champagne variant: To each bottle

add one bottle of club soda, one pony of brandy, one pony of Triple Sec, and the rind of one orange. Chill with large chunks of ice. Decorate with slices of fresh orange and pineapple, and sprigs of mint. Crushed fresh strawberries add a piquant flavor, or they may be left whole in the punch for guests to capture and munch. This will serve from twelve to sixteen guests.

The strawberry theme is a very popular one. Here is the ultimate concoction: Take two pounds of berries, cover well with sugar, add a pint of champagne, and let stand at room temperature for six hours. Then place a large chunk of ice in the punch bowl, and pour over it the strawberry liqueur thus concocted and a twenty-six-ounce bottle of chilled champagne. Add two ounces of curaçao and, when the liquid begins to blush an inviting pink, serve. This will serve from about ten to twelve guests.

Simple and supreme is the mixture of champagne and sherbet. Place a quart of lemon or pineapple sherbet in the punch bowl; pour two bottles of champagne, one bottle of sauterne, over the sherbet. Each drink is served with a dollop of sherbet. Serves eighteen.

And finally, the punch with the flavor to please all. Take one bottle of sherry, one bottle of brandy, one bottle of sauterne, and pour into the bowl, stirring to blend. Add a large chunk of ice. Stir until cold and add three bottles of champagne just when you are ready to serve. This will serve forty guests.

Long life and a happy one to the newlyweds!

She muses over music

It is as easy to picture spring without flowers as a wedding without music. Almost as important to a wedding as the words of the ritual, it bespeaks more clearly than words the gaiety, the solemnity, the romantic emotions gathered in one scene when two people walk forth into the great experiment of life. This cannot be said in words, but it can be felt in the music that has become an indispensable part of a wedding whether it is in a cathedral or the home of a bride. Melody has a way of moving in and taking possession of the scene. Musical compositions have a talent for appropriating for their own certain pictures and events. When music harmonizes with the scene, it acts as a unifying force to the events taking place. What all of us love and all of us know by heart is the music that gives delight at a wedding or at any other place where people are enjoying themselves. Music is a chameleon, taking its color from the people who are listening to it. It accelerates the mood; it dominates without one's being conscious of it. It moves people, puts them in unison with the setting of which they are a part.

Selection of music for a wedding is probably the most easily handled business on a bride's list of things to be done ahead of time, but there are taboos that must be observed. In many churches there is a growing resistance to certain music which is secular in origin as well as in the words associated with it. This is often not an exclusion by a specific denomination, but a bar raised by the pastor of a church within the denomination. It usually arises from an intense belief in the importance of the wedding ceremony and its sacred quality. Some of this conviction rests on no sound foundation, for music has a universal quality and many a hymn is based on a theme of folk music, or has been associated so emphatically with the wedding ceremony that many persons think of it only in that connection. A case in point is the "Bridal Chorus" from the third act of *Lohengrin*, used for half a century and more for the wedding Processional, followed by the tender exultation of the "Wedding March" from Mendelssohn's *Midsummer Night's Dream* for the Recessional.

In discussing the immemorial quality of these two musical masterpieces, Meyer Davis says, "It seems little short of destiny that there should be a wedding march for the Recessional entirely equal to the *Lohengrin* 'Bridal Chorus.' Mendelssohn's 'Wedding March' is no anticlimax to the inspiration in spirit of the bridal music from *Lohengrin*. Played by organ, orchestra or trio, the first is the perfect march to the altar, and the second dramatizes the future of a girl looking womanhood in the face. For a wedding within or outside a church, you have perfect music for two important phases of a wedding. In all my experience, I have never heard other than these two wedding marches whatever the church or denomination."

And it is true that these two wedding marches are banned by very few churches today. It is the triumph of splendid music, markedly secular in origin, fitting in magnificently in spirit with the rite of marriage so that its origin is not remembered by those who hear it. Where the wedding is a large one, and bridal funds are generous, the wedding procession headed by the full choir in its vestments singing the magnificent "Bridal Chorus" from *Lohengrin* may be a glorious prelude to the ceremony.

Now and then a clergyman wishing to eliminate all traces of the secular from services in his church may suggest to about-to-be brides "The King of Love My Shepherd Is," or "Praise My Soul, the King of Heaven," instead of the more usual marches. If all guests are members of the particular congregation, and are familiar with the practice, they will recognize the music that heralds the arrival of the bride. When the Queen of England, then Princess Elizabeth, was married to Lieutenant Philip Mountbatten, she chose to discard the traditional "Bridal Chorus" from *Lohengrin* in favor of a wedding march composed by Sir Hubert Parry in 1888. She moved with the groom into the sanctuary as the hymn "Praise My Soul, the King of Heaven" was sung. The hymn, composed by the Reverend H. F. Lyte, who also wrote "Abide with Me," was sung at the wedding of her parents. But the royal couple walked back down the aisle like any other couple, to the strains of the Mendelssohn "Wedding March." Catholic brides find that *The Nuptial Suite* of Albert Renaud and the *Wedding Music* of Father Carlo Rossini are both beautiful and acceptable to the Catholic clergy.

Beyond the wedding marches, taste and personal liking are the guiding rules for the music before and during the ceremony. As a matter of practical procedure, a bride should consult the musical director of her church, or the pastor, or both, in regard to the musical program for her wedding. They know the customs and musical taboos that must be respected.

The musical repertoire suitable to weddings is almost limitless. Meyer Davis gives a selection from a long list that is approved: "At the Altar," Arenski; "Be Thou but Near"; *Arioso in E Flat*; cantatas of Bach, especially "Jesu, Joy of Man's Desiring"; "Romance sans

Paroles," Bonnet; "My Inmost Heart Rejoiceth," Brahms; selections from *Messe de Mariage* of Dubois; Caesar Franck's *Cantabile* and *Pastorale; Arioso in D Major* of Handel; *Prelude in G* of Purcell; "Blessed Be the God and Father," Samuel Sebastian Wesley; *Andante*

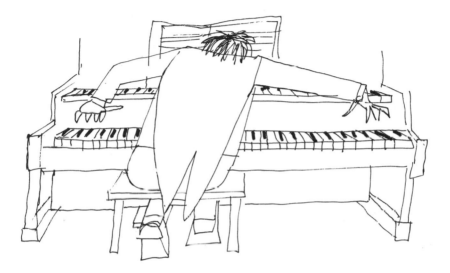

Cantabile by Widor; the Bach-Gounod "Ave Maria"; and the Schubert "Ave Maria." And many, many more.

Mr. Davis's selection of vocal solos starts with "The Voice That Breathed o'er Eden" by Haydn, and includes Burleigh's "O Perfect Love," Bach's "Be Thou but Near" and "Thou Art Like unto a Flower" by Robert Schumann and De Koven's "O, Promise Me."

In a wedding at home or at a hotel or club, musical selection has greater scope, and much music considered secular by churchmen may be used. Such as Walther's "Prize Song" from *Die Meistersinger,* the "Liebestod" from *Tristan und Isolde,* Wagner's "Traume" and "Oh, Thou Sublime Evening Star," "Meditation" from *Thaïs,* by Massenet, songs of Brahms, Schubert, Schumann, and Liszt's "Liebestraum," to name a very few.

MUSIC FOR THE WEDDING RECEPTION

At a wedding reception currently popular melodies are correct, but says Mr. Davis, "Out of long and sometimes bitter experience, I would advise intelligent censorship of popular songs. Certain delightful melodies must be eliminated because their titles do not fit the occasion. Language is something one must take into consideration. Words may neutralize an entrancing tune. My experience tells me that the desires of most people are answered in the music all of us know by heart. Brides ask me to play again and again such perennials as: Rubinstein's 'Melody in F,' Brahms' 'Lullaby,' Schubert's 'Serenade,' and such melodies of Victor Herbert as 'Kiss Me Again,' and 'Ah, Sweet Mystery of Life,' 'My Heart at Thy Sweet Voice,' and 'The Swan' of Saint-Saëns; 'Valse Bluette' by Drigo, the waltzes of Johann Strauss, Godard's 'Berceuse,' 'Poème' by Fibich, Boldi's 'Chanson Bohémienne,' 'Orientale' by Cui, 'Drink to Me Only with Thine Eyes,' and all the lovely music old and new, that we have grown to love. I am asked to play them all."

SIZE OF MUSICAL ENSEMBLE

The size of the musical ensemble is a matter of how many are to be entertained and the portion of the budget allotted to music. There may be three pieces or a full orchestra. Trios with a portable organ for background provide satisfactory music for a wedding at home with the reception following. They take up little space, when space is a point, and may be tucked under a staircase, in a foyer, or on the landing of a staircase if it is broad enough. Trios are perfect for wedding receptions in a suite of parlors at a hotel. Five to ten musicians are a good average group for most large receptions where there is dancing, but they must be experienced musicians used to playing request numbers.

A bride may be reassured by always remembering that music accommodates itself to any scene and any gathering. Music that touches her heart, music that seems apropos to her at this great moment, will be the music that awakens an echo in the heart of everyone sharing that moment with her.

She displays her presents

A happy tradition, part of the wedding reception in a bride's own home, is the display of her presents. Wedding presents are a tangible and spontaneous expression of the good will and affection everyone feels toward a bride, and to show them is the bride's expression of her own pleasure in receiving them. Now and then prosaic and matter-of-fact carpers criticize this happy custom, basing it upon a theoretical comparison between an opulent present, such as silver tea service, perhaps, and a small gift of china or glass or silver. A sounder reason for a lessening of this agreeable custom is the increased use of hotels and clubs for the reception. Today's small apartments and houses make it difficult to set aside a room for the display of presents, but when it is possible it is a highlight of a reception at home, second only to the wedding cake. The bride may mark the occasion with a luncheon, tea, cocktail party, or dinner.

On the other hand, there is a growing feeling that cards of donors should not be displayed beside their gifts, and if a gift list is correctly kept, it is not necessary. In any event checks are never identified nor displayed. Instead there is a prevalent method used by many brides to scatter among the gifts small white cards on which is written the word "check," followed by the amount. It is far simpler, we think, for a member of the family showing presents to say something like "Uncle Jim sent Clare a lovely check. They are going to use it for the living-room draperies." Nevertheless, if it is a local custom to show cards, it is perfectly correct to do so. As gifts are received they should be kept in one room. The present should be immediately entered in the gift list. Thank-you notes, which need not be long, should be sent without delay. Telephoned or verbal thanks are not sufficient for friends who have gone to the trouble to select and send a present. An engraved card of acknowledgment with the information that the bride will write a note later does not meet the situation. It is neither adequate nor courteous. In acknowledging a joint gift of a man and wife, the bride writes to the wife, thanking both.

Exchange of duplicate gifts is entirely proper. It is expected nowadays. No feelings are hurt or should be.

She has her picture taken

Most brides like to have their picture taken. It is the high point of their emotional life; it is the moment of greatest beauty. At least these are the traditions, and if they are not exactly the literal truth, they are close enough to it to be accepted.

There will probably be photographs taken at the wedding itself, and at the parties, as part of the record. These will show the bride and her gown from many angles, but it is usually a good idea to have a formal portrait taken in the studio. The bride's parents treasure such a portrait, and the groom himself will want to keep it close to him through his life. Another practical consideration is that a studio portrait may be taken early enough to be released to the newspapers for their announcement at the time of the wedding. This means, of course, that the bride's gown and veil should be finished in time for the portrait.

Even in this practical age, it is considered bad luck for the groom to see his bride in her gown before the ceremony itself. Therefore the bride should arrange to have him at a distance when she is dressing for her portrait and sitting at the studio. Who's superstitious today? But why not play along all the way in the age-old marriage game? There is charm in much make-believe, and wisdom in other superstitions. It may not hurt to see a bride, but it surely reduces the chances of being beaned by falling objects when you avoid walking under ladders. So let's not get married on the thirteenth, and let's not peek at the bride.

She remembers cars, canopies, and photographers

The bride's family, as the host family, will do everything possible for the convenience and comfort of their guests. This can vary in degree, according to the circumstances and formality of the wedding. But there are certain minimum considerations.

One is transportation. The day is over when the bride's father might feel it incumbent upon him to supply automobile transport for everyone in the party. There will be, however, certain ones present who should have limousines hired for the occasion—specifically, the bride and groom, the attendants and ushers, the parents. There should probably be an extra car or two for other honored or perhaps aged guests. Otherwise, there will be plenty of guests arriving in their own automobiles which will be available for picking up out-of-towners who arrived by plane or train—that is, picking them up at the church and transporting them to the reception. A thoughtful host will assign one or two cars for all-day-and-night duty on the day preceding the wedding and, during the wedding day, to reach incoming guests at station or airport and to get them to the wedding or the reception as they arrive.

A canopy should be erected outside the church, to protect the married couple, the wedding party, and all the guests, in case of inclement weather. The same should apply at the place where the reception is to be held—club, hotel, or home. If an outdoor reception is planned and there is some suspicion that a driving rain would tax the capacity of the indoor quarters available, a covered pavilion or tent should be provided to protect the guests. Such equipment is available in the bride's home community, but it should be reserved for use considerably ahead of time.

The bride has already had her picture taken, formally, in the studio, but a photographer should be engaged to shoot candids of the whole happy occasion as it progresses. The bride is pictured as she descends the staircase in her home, attired in her wedding gown. Other members of the family are photographed leaving the house. The scenes in the church may be discreetly photographed, but in accordance with the wishes of the clergyman in this matter. Leaving the church, arriving at the reception, the bridal table, the dancing; every joyous scene is recorded. The photographer is given special instructions to make certain that close friends or important guests are photographed as well as members of the bridal party itself. The photographer is also given special instructions as to the nature of his job: he is there to work, not to make merry; a clear head results in clear pictures.

The photographs make a record which will give the wedded pair many hours of delight, reminiscence, and amusement during the years of their life ahead. Made into an album, there are few more precious mementos of a wedding.

This tradition is a rewarding "must."

One word of warning. Well-meaning amateurs, or camera bugs in the family, should be kindly but firmly excluded from performing this service. An experienced professional, reputable and predictable, is the only possible choice. It will happen only once in a lifetime, and no mistakes or omissions should be permitted.

She perfects her wedding etiquette

THE WEDDING REHEARSAL

Is a rehearsal of the wedding necessary? It is if the wedding is to be a large one with a number of bridesmaids and ushers, and espe-

cially if there are to be junior bridesmaids, flower girls, or a ring bearer in the bridal party.

The Processional and Recessional especially must be rehearsed. It should be borne in mind that both are marches, the Recessional paced to a bit quicker tempo than the Processional. Before the Processional is rehearsed, it must be decided where bridesmaids, ushers, and other members of the cast are to stand during the ceremony, so that when the Processional is first stepped off to music they will know where to go as they approach the chancel.

It follows that the organist must be present at the rehearsal.

Each pair follows the couple directly in front of it by four paces—that is, four beats of time. The bride with her father counts eight beats before she puts her *left* foot forward.

In a rehearsal, the place of the bride is filled by a substitute. The bride herself takes no part other than to observe and probably make suggestions. No words of the service are spoken, the clergyman merely indicating his part in the ceremony and directing others.

It is altogether a simple and painless, though essential, prelude to a perfect wedding.

THE FORMAL CHURCH WEDDING

Punctuality is the word that dominates the wedding day until the ceremony is over and the newly married pair have left the church. A time chart for synchronizing the movements of the bridal party on the day of the wedding would look something like this:

Ushers arrive at the church one hour before the ceremony. There they receive their boutonnieres, which have been delivered by the florist to the sexton.

Bridesmaids arrive at the home of the bride not less than a half hour before the bridal party is to leave for the church. There they receive their bouquets. At this time candid shots may be taken of the maids alone and with the bride.

The mother of the bride leaves for the church. She may take several bridesmaids in her car. Other bridesmaids follow in one or more cars.

The bride and her father follow.

The groom's mother and father, in the meantime, have left for the church, timing their arrival about four or five minutes before the bride's mother.

As soon as the bride's mother enters the vestibule of the church, the head usher escorts the mother of the groom to her place in the first pew on the right side, her husband following closely after. The usher returns immediately for the bride's mother, who is the last person to be seated before the entrance of the bride.

The entrance of the bride's mother is a signal. Immediately after she arrives, the white bridal carpet, if one is used, is unrolled.

The bride and her father arrive, and the doors of the church are closed. The bridal party is ready for the Processional.

The ceremony now starts. The opening peal of the wedding march is the cue for the clergyman, followed by the groom and best man, to enter the chancel.

The groom walks to the head of the aisle, and stands on the right side to await his bride. (*Note:* Right, when used in reference to the church, means the right side as the congregation faces the altar.) He removes his right glove and places it in his left hand or passes it to his best man. He may remove both gloves, and hand them to his best man, who will put them in his own pocket. In either case his right hand must be bare when he takes his bride's hand and draws it into the crook of his arm.

The best man remains back and to the right of the groom. He does not remove his gloves.

The bridal procession always forms in the vestibule and enters the aisle from that point. As the first bar of the wedding march sounds, the ushers enter and step forward in time with the music, four paces apart. They have previously been matched according to height, with the shortest pair first. The bridesmaids, who have also been paired according to height, follow in the same sequence of height. After them comes the maid, or matron, of honor, walking alone. A flower girl, if any, immediately precedes the bride; a ring bearer should precede the flower girl by the same four paces that separate the pairs of bridal attendants.

Last comes the bride, walking with her father, her left hand on his right arm. (This position brings her closest to her groom when she reaches the chancel steps and enables her father to step to the left and, after he has given his daughter away, unobtrusively to reach the pew where his wife sits.)

In certain situations the bride may elect to walk alone. If she so chooses, she is given away by her mother, who answers the clergy-

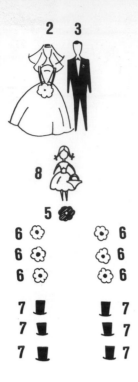

2   3

8

5

6   6

6   6

6   6

7   7

7   7

7   7

Key to Wedding Chart

1. Clergyman
2. Bride
3. Groom
4. Best Man
5. Maid of Honor
6. Bridesmaids
7. Ushers
8. Flower Girl
9. Bride's Father
10. Bride's Mother
11. Groom's Father
12. Groom's Mother

PROCESSIONAL

Diagrams indicate positions of the wedding party as they move toward the altar and as they turn from the altar for the recessional.

6   7

6   7

6   7

6   7

6   7

6   7

5   4

8

2   3

RECESSIONAL

Ushers and bridesmaids may use positions indicated in recessional diagram or march in the same order as in the processional.

At the Altar

The exact position of the wedding party at the altar is shown in the diagram.

Reception

Positions of members of the wedding party in the receiving line. Frequently neither father stands in the line; the bride's father as host looking after guests, the groom's father participating in the festivities.

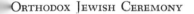

Orthodox Jewish Ceremony

In the Orthodox Jewish ceremony the wedding party stands under the canopy in accordance with the key. Ushers and bridesmaids stand outside the canopy; maids on the bride's, side ushers on the side of the groom.

Bride's Table

Who's who at the bride's table. The numbers refer to the chart above. At a large wedding, the parents of both bride and groom are seated at another table.

man's question "Who giveth this woman?" from where she stands in the front pew on the left. In this rare instance it is important for the bride's mother to rehearse with the other members of the bridal party and to answer promptly on cue. The more usual procedure of having a brother, uncle, or close friend of the family serve in place of an absent father is better.

To summarize, this is the order of the Processional:
1. Ushers, two by two
2. Bridesmaids, two by two
3. Matron, or maid, of honor, alone
4. Ring bearer, alone
5. Flower girl, alone
6. Bride and her father

POSITIONS OF BRIDE AND ATTENDANTS AT ALTAR

When the bride reaches the head of the aisle where the groom is waiting, she withdraws her hand from her father's arm. He remains where she leaves him. Changing her bouquet from her right to her left arm, she places her right hand in the arm of the groom, and they face the altar together.

The matron, or maid, of honor, takes her position one step back and to the left of the bride. The best man's place is one step back of the groom and to the right.

The ushers divide at the foot of the chancel. In a small church the first pair ascends the chancel steps and stand at the top, one usher to the right, the other on the left. The second two stop a step below. If there are more, they stand below. In a large church, the ushers go farther up the steps, or all of them stand in front of the choir stalls.

The bridesmaids divide as they reach the chancel, half to the right, half to the left, and stand in front of the ushers. It is not correct, nor is the effect agreeable, for all bridesmaids to range themselves on the side of the bride and all ushers on that of the groom.

A flower girl stands to the left, near the honor attendant; the ring bearer near the best man, who will remove the ring from the cushion when it is time for him to give it to the groom.

The organist ceases playing the moment bride and groom take their places. It matters not whether she rests her hand in his arm or whether

they stand hand in hand or merely side by side as they face the clergyman.

THE MARRIAGE CEREMONY

The clergyman, standing a step or two above the bride and groom, reads the betrothal.

When he says, "Who giveth this woman to be married?" the father, who has been waiting a step or two behind the bride and to her left, moves forward on the left until he is beside her. The bride turns slightly toward her father and gives him her right hand. The father puts her hand in that of the clergyman, and says, "I do." He then leaves and goes to the side of his wife—who is always in the first pew on the left—taking the place next to the aisle.

The clergyman ascends to the altar. The bride and groom go slowly after him, the fingers of her right hand on the groom's arm. The maid

of honor steps out of line and follows on the left side until she stands immediately below the bride. The best man takes the same relative position on the right side of the groom. The ring bearer, if any, also moves forward. The flower girl retains her position.

The bride hands her bouquet to the maid of honor—if she carries a prayer book, she hands it to the clergyman—and the bride and groom plight their troth.

At the proper moment in the ceremony, the best man takes the wedding ring from his pocket, or from the ring bearer, and hands it to the groom, who passes it to the clergyman. It is blessed by the clergyman and returned to the groom, who slips it on the ring finger of the bride's left hand. Previous to the ceremony she removed her engagement ring, which may be replaced after the ceremony, worn over the wedding ring.

With the conclusion of the ritual, the minister congratulates the wedded pair. At this point the groom may kiss the bride or not. In some churches the kiss is frowned on, so it is wise to know the views of the clergyman who conducts the ceremony on whether it is approved. At weddings at home a kiss is always proper, but in any case it should be only a token gesture.

THE RECESSIONAL

The organ bursts into the march for the Recessional. The bride receives her bouquet from her maid of honor. She turns toward her husband—her bouquet is in her right hand—and she puts her left hand through his right arm. They descend the steps.

The Recessional is exactly the reverse of the Processional. The order is:

1. Bride and groom, together
2. Flower girl, alone
3. Ring bearer, alone
4. Honor attendant, alone
5. Bridesmaids, two by two
6. Ushers, two by two

It is permissible for ushers and bridesmaids to walk in the Recessional in pairs, and it has become a customary sight at most of today's weddings; but many people believe that the picture is not only more charming, but more dignified, if the older order of bridesmaids in pairs and ushers in pairs is followed. The bride, however, has the decision in this formality, as she has in every other matter affecting her wedding.

At the close of the wedding ritual the best man returns to the vestry, where he gathers together the belongings of the groom and hurries to the entrance of the church to give them to him. He then returns to the vestry to hand the clergyman his fee, and then hastens to the bride's home or wherever the reception is being held. *Note:* One of the sexton's aides may take the groom's coat, hat, and stick to him at the front of the church while the best man sees the minister in the vestry.

The Recessional march over, ushers return and escort to the entrance of the church all ladies seated in the front pews. The bride's mother first; the groom's mother next. Then other guests in the front pews on both sides of the aisle follow.

Guests at a large wedding remain in their seats until all members of the immediate families have left the church.

ORDER OF LEAVING THE CHURCH

Motorcars leave the front of the church in the following order:

1. Bride's car, with bride and groom
2. Bridesmaids
3. Parents of the bride
4. Parents of the groom
5. Remaining cars carry immediate families of the bride and groom, clergyman, ushers, and other guests

It is correct for several bridesmaids to ride in the cars of parents of the bride and groom after the ceremony, and this is often done. But it is an infallible rule that bride and groom ride alone.

THE WEDDING RECEPTION

The hour of the wedding reception is necessarily keyed to the hour of the wedding ceremony; it should be set for immediately after it. A morning or noon wedding calls for a wedding breakfast to follow at once. Guests may be seated, or it may be a buffet meal. For an afternoon ceremony a reception is correct. A wedding taking place in the evening calls for a supper or a reception.

THE RECEIVING LINE

The mother of the bride, who is the formal hostess, greets all guests as they arrive at the reception, breakfast, or supper. She may stand at the door of the room accompanied by the mother of the groom, to whom guests who are strangers to her are introduced. The

father of the groom may stand with them also, but a practical and proper alternative is for the father of the bride to introduce guests to the groom's father after the guests have passed the receiving line. A practical pattern for this is:

1. Mothers of bride and groom at door of reception room
2. Bridesmaids
3. Flower girl, if any, and if she is old enough to play the part
4. Groom
5. Bride
6. Maid of honor
7. Bridesmaids

In this plan, fathers of bride and groom do not "receive," but circulate about among guests. It also expedites the passage of guests by the receiving line, a tiring though agreeable as well as necessary feature of any wedding festivity.

Best man and ushers should be busy among the guests, making themselves useful and affable.

When a seated breakfast or supper is served, the bridal party remains in line until guests have passed and almost everyone is in the dining room. By this time the second course is being served. Arm in arm, the bride and groom move to the bridal table followed by the rest of the bridal party.

If the breakfast is a buffet meal, the receiving line remains until all guests have passed. The ushers then escort the bridesmaids to the dining room.

THE SEATING AT THE BRIDE'S TABLE

This has been taken up before, in the section on the etiquette of the groom and his best man, but it is worth repeating here. (See chart on page 141.)

The bride sits in the center of the table, to the right of the groom. To her right is the best man. To his right is a bridesmaid and then, alternately, ushers and bridesmaids. To the left of the groom is the maid of honor, to her left, an usher, and then, alternately, bridesmaids and ushers, with perhaps wives and husbands of these attendants mingled in. At a large wedding, the parents of both bride and groom are seated at another table, with some of the older guests and, of course, the officiating clergyman.

WHEN THERE IS DANCING

Once the receiving line has broken, custom decrees that bride and groom, without variation, have the first dance together. No one takes the floor until this solo flight has gone on for a few turns, usually accompanied by applause from guests. It is the cue for dancing to become general.

In today's pattern for this first dance of the newly married pair, the bride's father is first to cut in on the dance. The groom's father follows, and then the best man will without fail. After him a bride will dance with the ushers and other guests.

The groom invites the bride's mother to dance, and after her his own mother. Without fail, he will dance with the maid of honor. The best man will also invite the mothers of bride and groom to dance.

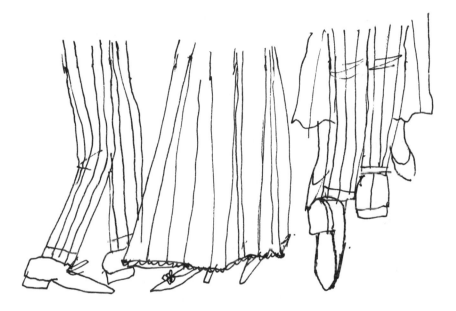

Unless the bride and groom have an inflexible date with a train or plane, they should stay until the crowd thins. At last the bride signals to the bridesmaids that she is about to leave the room to go upstairs. As they gather at the foot of the stairs, the bride pauses halfway to the floor above and tosses her bouquet for the bridesmaids to attempt to catch. The one who succeeds, legend has it, will be the next to be a bride. If the reception takes place in an apartment or hotel ballroom, the old custom may still be observed, even if the bride merely tosses her bouquet from a distance of eight or ten feet to her maids.

The bride goes to the room where she is to change. Her mother, sisters, and bridesmaids gather with her while she puts on her going-away suit.

When the bride has left the groom, he goes to a room reserved for him and changes from formal clothes. Having changed he waits in the hall until his bride joins him. It is at this point that a thoughtful bride has sent for the groom's mother so that they may say good-by to her. This is especially important if the groom's mother is a stranger.

The bride's mother gives her daughter a last kiss. The bridesmaids station themselves near the front door; then the newlyweds run the gauntlet of rice and/or rose-petal tossers, reach their car, slam the door, and are off, a completely wedded couple by bell, book, and well-observed custom.

WHEN THE WEDDING IS NOT IN CHURCH

Given the chance, most brides elect to be married in church. It obviously accents the sanctity of the marriage rites. But practical reasons of many kinds often dictate a wedding ceremony elsewhere.

Clubs and hotels are a bride's home-away-from-home in today's scheme of things. Hotels now take care of so many weddings that they usually keep altars and canopies on hand to convert a small ballroom into a very acceptable chapel. Having ceremony and reception under one roof offers definite saving advantages of time and expense.

Next to a marriage in church, the wedding at home is in the best American tradition. An old-fashioned house makes a beautiful background for the bridal scene, but any home may be the scene for a charming wedding.

And there is scarcely a home too small to be the setting for a dignified wedding that will not let a bride's dreams down. Planning will do it. In a house large or small the layout must be held well in mind, for the spot chosen for the ceremony is the point from which every other detail and arrangement will follow. This spot should be where the line of march moves forward without halt or crowding, first to the ceremony, then to the receiving line, and finally to the bridal buffet.

Visualize clearly where guests will stand to form an aisle for the

Processional. This is more than half the solution of the wedding-at-home problem. Do not try to set up an altar, for room is likely to be a consideration. Make a setting with tall floor vases of flowers, or trimmed floor candelabra, but space is usually too valuable for more. If the service calls for it, provide a low hassock or bench for kneeling.

The home ceremony is seldom followed by a Recessional. After the benediction, the groom invariably kisses his bride and they turn from the clergyman to receive the congratulations of their guests. The receiving line at such a reception will be less formal than at a hotel or club. The maid of honor will stand with bride and groom, and if there are bridesmaids they also will be part of the receiving line.

If folding seats have been provided for the wedding guests, they are quickly removed as soon as the ceremony is over in order not to impede the movement to and away from the receiving line.

A garden wedding is a beautiful expression of the wedding at home. It should be attempted only if the garden is spacious enough to provide an appropriate spot for the ceremony and scope for the bridal procession. Many attractive features may be created, such as an improvised altar against a trellis or arbor, or pergola. The flowers, especially of the months of May and June, furnish an unrivaled natural setting. But it is well to provide a well-thought-out alternative setting indoors in case of rain or an overcast sky. If the garden is large enough, a canopy spacious enough to shelter the entire party may be set up as absolute rain-insurance.

THE DOUBLE WEDDING

In double weddings the usual conventionalities and appointments are multiplied by two. Special problems that arise are solved according to the type of wedding, and to individual taste. Each bridal pair has their own attendants. In the wedding procession all ushers come first, and they are followed by the bridesmaids of the older bride, her maid of honor, the bride herself on her father's arm. If the two brides are sisters, the younger bride is escorted by a brother, uncle, or cousin, but both brides will be given away by their father. Then comes the party of the younger bride, in exactly the same order, ushers excepted; they, as stated, having gone ahead.

Sisters sometimes choose to share the bridesmaids, the group being made up of friends of both. In this instance *all* bridesmaids follow the ushers. The following is the pattern for this bridal procession: all ushers, all bridesmaids, honor attendant of the older bride, the bride on her father's arm; honor attendant of the younger bride, bride on her brother's arm.

Both brides are met by their grooms in the usual fashion. Both pairs stand side by side in front of the clergyman, the older pair to the right, the younger to the left. The precedence of the Processional is observed in the Recessional.

If the brides are not sisters, friendliness is indicated by a double wedding; hence the parents of both grooms would sit in the front right pew, the parents of the older bride's groom nearest the aisle. If parents of the younger bride's groom prefer, they may sit in the second left pew.

Brides at a double wedding need not be dressed alike, nor do their respective groups of attendants, though in both instances it is desirable to have all clothes similar as to length and general type.

Invitations to a formal double wedding, except that they carry two sets of names, are the same in form as for any other wedding.

THE MILITARY WEDDING

So colorful and dramatic is the military wedding that it is likely to be favored when the groom is in a branch of the armed forces, and a military wedding in time of peace is marked by the highest formality once a bride chooses to make hers a formal wedding. A military wedding requires every member of the armed forces to be in dress uniform. Civilians wear formal morning dress for a daytime wedding; white tie and tails for an evening wedding.

When the groom is in the regular Army, his regimental flag, together with the Colors (the American flag in parlance of the military), may sometimes be placed in the chancel. With the flowers and

candles the flags make a colorful background for the wedding ceremony, which is pretty impressive on its own account.

Guests are seated in accordance with military protocol governing
rank. For instance, if the groom's commanding officer and his wife

are present, they are seated in the pew directly behind the groom's
mother and father.

The military wedding ceremony differs in no respect from the
service at a civilian wedding. The Processional and Recessional and
grouping of bridal attendants in the chancel follow the customary
order.

Next to the glamour and pageantry of uniforms, another difference is
in the famous arch of swords. It usually takes place outside the church
door—always outside at Episcopalian and Catholic weddings—extending down the church steps. If exigencies of weather or heavy traffic

make it preferable, the arch is formed in the vestibule of the church. Only the bride and groom walk under the arch of sabers.

Military ushers may stand at attention in two facing lines at the entrance of the church after the ceremony until all guests have passed between, while the bride and groom wait in the vestibule. After this they form the arch of swords for the bride and groom.

Reserve officers may wear their field service uniforms, even for an evening wedding, and it is quite likely that they will continue to do so while they hold their reserve officer's commission. Best man and ushers will wear the same style of uniform, with the correct insignia for reserve officers. This means that at evening weddings of reserve officers, civilian men will wear dinner coats and women evening dresses.

THE ROMAN CATHOLIC WEDDING

Except for strictly religious mandates, formal weddings in Catholic churches have much the same protocol as Protestant weddings. In appearance the Processional and Recessional are essentially alike: ushers come first in pairs; the bridesmaids in pairs follow; then the maid of honor; and the bride on the left arm of her father.

There are two notable exceptions. If the wedding is solemnized by a Nuptial Mass, bridesmaids and ushers at the conclusion of the Processional go to seats reserved for them immediately behind the parents of bride and groom: maid of honor and bridesmaids to the left, best man and ushers to the right. There they remain during the Mass until they join bride and groom at the altar rail to receive Holy Communion. The other exception is that, though the Catholic father escorts his daughter to the foot of the chancel, where she meets the bridegroom, he leaves her and immediately joins his wife in their pew. He does not give his daughter away, as it is not part of the Catholic ritual. *Note:* Many people, even Catholics, confuse the escorting of the bride by her father with the act of giving her away, but there are no words in the Catholic ritual corresponding to those of the betrothal of the Protestant service. Technically, of course, when he turns his daughter over to the groom at the chancel, it is symbolically an act of giving her away.

The Catholic wedding is most often celebrated with a Nuptial Mass. The Solemn Nuptial Mass is the most elaborate of wedding ceremonies. It uses a full choir and its ritual requires three priests, each of whom sings a part of the Mass. There are a celebrant, a deacon, and a subdeacon.

The Missa Cantata is a high Mass that takes about forty minutes and, of course, is mostly sung. The low Nuptial Mass, which takes a half hour, is much used. Any Nuptial Mass is said only for those being married for the first time and contains special prayers and a special ritual.

Weddings with low Mass at ten o'clock are quite usual, and weddings at eight o'clock in the morning are not at all rare. Many Catholic weddings are celebrated in the afternoon (naturally without Mass) in a simple ceremony. Elaborate formal weddings take place at noon.

The marriage of two Catholics normally must take place in the parish church of the bride. If, however, for important reasons a bride and groom wish to marry outside the bride's parish, they must furnish credentials of baptism and written proof of their freedom to wed.

The marriage may take place in church, at home, or at a club or hotel. For a wedding outside the church, special permission of the bishop must be obtained.

The marriage of two Catholics requires that banns be proclaimed from the churches of bride and groom respectively if they live in different parishes, on three successive Sundays before the wedding. In the case of the groom banns must be read at every church of which he has been a communicant from the age of sixteen.

In mixed marriages—marriages between a non-Catholic and a Catholic—the wedding may take place in a church or cathedral by permission of the bishop of the diocese. If the marriage is to be between an unbaptized person and a Catholic, dispensation from Rome must be secured. The marriage of a Catholic and non-Catholic, though it takes place in church, is not solemnized within the sanctuary but outside the altar rails. Witnesses—that is, the maid of honor and best man—must be Catholic. Banns are not read if either bride or groom is non-Catholic.

THE JEWISH WEDDING

There is much of the Old World left in the Jewish wedding in this country, but inroads of American manners and protocol of the bridal party are more and more apparent as the Jewish wedding moves from Orthodox to Reform. Nevertheless, these weddings must remain Jewish in spirit and traditional ceremony.

Orthodox or Reform, the wedding may be held in a temple or at home, or anywhere else the bride and her family elect to hold it. It has been popular practice for large Jewish weddings to take place in a hall or the ballroom of a hotel or club, in town or country. The canopy ("*chupeh*") and the goblets as well as other ceremonial articles are easily provided wherever the wedding is held. The *chupeh* is used in some congregations and omitted by others.

In the marriage ceremony, certain portions are read in English, and the several blessings, though always read first in Hebrew, are translated by the officiating rabbi into English. If the wedding is in a temple, men guests frequently do not wear hats, and they and women guests sit together, contrary to the custom at Orthodox Jewish religious ceremonies.

The bride and groom are given away by the parents of each. Either parental couple, however, may be represented by another married couple if the mother and father are unable to be present.

The marriage is always symbolized by the wedding ring. The groom slides it on the finger of the bride, but on the index finger of the right hand. The bride transfers it later to the third finger of the left hand. Practice, however, varies in some congregations.

Part of the ceremonial equipment necessary at every Jewish wedding, Reform or Orthodox, is a small table bearing a decanter of wine and glasses. One of these is a thin glass wrapped in a cloth or napkin. The bride and groom drink from a glass of wine as part of the ceremony. The thin glass handed to the groom by the rabbi is placed on the floor and broken under his heel.

The Reform ceremony is brief, taking about ten minutes. After it the rabbi delivers a short address to the married pair, reminding them of their new duties and responsibilities.

The Orthodox ceremony is strict in adherence to ancient Jewish pattern. The canopy is always used, and the service is read in Hebrew and a portion in Aramaic embodying the pledge of fidelity of the groom to the bride, and the bride's obligations to the new household. When the ceremony takes place in a synagogue, men wear their hats and sit apart from the women.

In many states, New York for instance, the portion of the ceremony in which there occurs the question "Dost thou take this woman to be thy wedded wife?" and the corresponding question to the bride are required by law to be read in English.

Variations of both the Orthodox and Reform ceremonies, it should be kept in mind, are found in different communities and in different congregations. The officiating rabbi and families discuss in advance the requirements and what is to take place.

Orthodox or Reform, a certificate of marriage is issued by the rabbi to the newly married pair, a document apart and distinct from the marriage license. In Hebrew, with translation into English, it contains the year and date according to the modern as well as the Hebrew calendar.

THE SECOND WEDDING

A second wedding should be no less joyful an occasion than a first, filled with hope and good wishes for the future.

The divorcée will probably prefer to be married at home or by a justice of the peace, avoiding the embarrassment of being advised, as is the case with so many churches, that there are rules against a church wedding which involves a divorced person. This rule is not *always* the case, so the preferred church may be investigated in advance, by discreet inquiry, if a church wedding is strongly desired by the couple.

Often the minister may be convinced of the sincerity and religious intent, of the couple and will waive the rule in their favor.

The young widow, if in her twenties, may have a formal church wedding or a semiformal wedding, but she should not wear white or have a veil or train. The procedures of the wedding ceremonies are the same as with a previously unmarried bride, but it is thought best to restrict the number of guests to a possible fifty or sixty and accordingly reduce the number of bridal attendants and ushers. The older widow will probably decide upon an informal church wedding or civil ceremony. The ceremony will usually be in private, with friends and relatives invited to the reception.

The groom's second marriage. The idea of a formal wedding is usually more in honor of the bride than of the groom, so that this is permissible if the bride has not been married before. Very often, under these circumstances or if both bride and groom have been married before, there are children on one or both sides. This involves delicate feelings, but the usual procedure is to leave it up to the children as to whether or not they may wish to attend the wedding. If they wish to attend, their presence is considered perfectly good form.

If you would be loved, love.

SENECA

Chapter Four

❦

And Happily Ever Afterward

A word to the wives

IN WRITING this book, most of the parts addressed to the groom were written by Mr. F.A.B., and the words to the bride by Mrs. F.A.B. But now the roles change. In the matter of what a man expects of a wife, Mr. B. has a word for the wives.

As in most things, what has been said about marriage—and there has been plenty—is quotable more on the negative than the positive side.

"The one charm of marriage is that it makes a life of deception absolutely necessary for both parties."

"Every woman should marry—and no man."

Robert Louis Stevenson pondered long and deeply about marriage and it was he who gave us the title for the lectures we gave all over the country, on "The Tender Battleground of Marriage." He wrote a passage that is sad and beautiful and wise:

"Marriage is a step so grave and decisive that it attracts light-headed, variable men by its very awfulness. They may have been so tried among the inconstant squalls and currents, so often sailed for islands in the air or lain becalmed with burning heart, that they will risk all for solid ground beneath their feet. . . . It seems as if marriage were the royal road through life, and realised, on the instant, what we have all dreamed on summer Sundays when the bells ring, or at night when we cannot sleep for the desire of living. They think it will sober and change them. Like those who join a brotherhood, they fancy that it needs but an act to be out of the coil and clamour forever. But this is a wile of the devil's. To the end, spring winds will sow disquietude, passing faces leave a regret behind them, and the whole world keep calling and calling in their ears. For marriage is like life in this—that it is a field of battle and not a bed of roses."

Of course, it must be admitted that the male and the female are vastly different in composition, even while we cry *vive la différence*. A woman has more phosphorus—not to mention other miscellaneous furniture—in her brain than a mere man. A woman needs less sleep. She needs different kinds of food. She has a more acute color sense. Her thermostatic controls are entirely different: she is able to keep warmer in winter, cooler in summer, than a man. The tiny patch on the left temporal lobe of her cortex, bordering on the fissure of Sylvius, is where her speech impulses come from—if any male is interested— and this spot of gray matter is inevitably in excellent working trim.

It is no wonder that there may be some differences in what time the couple should go to bed, how wide open the window should be, and the like. But these are details of living that any loving people can easily control. The real monsters lying in wait for the newly married couple are more horrendous, as well as more predictable. Let me tick off a few of them.

I would say that most men, and I use the word with care, dislike bossiness in a wife more than anything else. A few mama's boys like to be told what to do all the time, and some of them will trade every shred of independence for the pleasures of being waited on and coddled. But a regular guy, the kind *you* married, likes to think that he is wedded to a girl and not a field marshal or chairman of the board. It is not masculine simple-mindedness that puts such girl types as Marilyn Monroe in the limelight. These girls represent a distillate of femininity which unfortunately seems to be becoming increasingly rare in our society. It is as simple as all that. A man never complains when he is "managed" through love; he just doesn't want to be on the receiving end of orders all the time, issued publicly or privately.

That shouldn't mean that a man expects to run the household purely to please himself, either. By and large, most husbands, and particularly young ones, don't object to doing all sorts of things that were formerly considered only woman's work—washing dishes, walking the baby, and the like. There are certain meals in our home that I always cook because I do them better than Fran, just as she specializes in others. But the point here is that a man likes to be regarded as a helper and not as the household answer to the disappearance of the servant class. He likes to be choosy about what he does in the line of household work, and if you want him to step into something you're pretty sure he doesn't like, it seems smarter to ask him than to order him.

A second source of unhappiness has to do with his friends. This is a touchy subject. A bachelor's pals are not always happy choices, from a new wife's point of view. They have the edge on her, frequently, in memories and shared experiences, and this can make her uncomfortable. And they frequently take liberties with "his" home without considering that it is also hers. The best advice for a young wife is for her to make a sincere effort to adopt her husband's friends as her own. If it doesn't work out, she should be frank in telling him the reasons why; perhaps he can arrange for some improvements. If not, he still should be free to see his friends, perhaps on his own, and the wife should be careful to make certain gestures that will keep the problem from being too sharply recognizable. A basic plan for newly-weds is to make new friends together, usually young couples who can share the same interests. Old friends of both the wife and the husband can often be introduced happily into this new circle, and a whole new relationship can be thus established.

Without trying to go too deeply into the marriage counseling bit, there are probably two habits of the modern young lady which are most annoying to the modern young man. Usually, he is in business by the time he is married, and he tends to think of the telephone as an instrument of communication, whereas many a girl considers it an instrument of amusement and relaxation. A girl who has spent years of her adolescence with a telephone to her ear, with the bills going to an indulgent father, may not understand how the habit can annoy her normally sensible young husband. It is almost sure to, however, especially if the calls are made to a female friend and the squeals, exclamation points, and confidences of "girl talk" are all that he can hear. A good rule is to keep the phone for communication during the evenings, and for amusement and relaxation when the breadwinner is out winning bread.

The other habit is equally innocuous. Men are not notoriously neat animals, they can throw clothes, ashes, and just plain junk around the house as if they planned to leave it forever in the next ten minutes. But men are also careful about where they leave things, and prefer to have a regular place for items like flashlights, bottle openers, and the like. It may sound silly, but informal surveys conducted on the subject indicate that one of the chief minor irritants of married life is the female tendency to leave caps off toothpaste tubes, tops off jars, and, especially, to squeeze a toothpaste tube (shared by husband and wife, in their favorite brand) completely at random, leaving it tortured and spent, with most of the paste at the bottom end.

The most difficult problem of all, of course, is Family. What the young wife must realize from the beginning is that her husband is apt to be quite free in criticizing his own family. In his own way, humorously or sharply or lovingly, or all three, he will have lots to say about them, and not all of it of a complimentary nature. But the young wife must beware of the trap. These sonlike observations are strictly for the man. If she even agrees with them, it is dangerous; but it is simply explosive if she makes any remarks of her own. Her best plan is to keep quiet on the subject of his family unless she has something complimentary to say. She must control her attitude as well: if she can find a way to love them, she is lucky; if she can find a way to get along with them at all times, she is wise. Her best plan of action is to concentrate on their virtues and find a way to enjoy them. Their defects do not exist, as far as she is concerned. That is the perfect and only plan for happiness-in-law.

Another trap is the one called human nature. Miss Candy Jones, the young lady famous for her "cover girl" career and now the director of her own school for teaching career girls how to be charming and effective, points up one of the unexpected results of a bride and groom being merely human:

"Well, finally you are back. Back from the two golden weeks in Bermuda, from the bicycling through the rattle-de-bang streets of Hamilton, from the hot apple pie at Waterlot Inn on the bay front, from the little lizards crawling along the curbstones and the beautiful flowers spilling all over everywhere.

"But are you sure you brought the right man back?

"He doesn't seem exactly the same, does he? The man you were with in Bermuda was William the Conqueror, Tab Hunter, the Shah of Iran, and a few others rolled into one. The Renaissance man. The most beautiful man. The man of sixteen cylinders, gentle and strong, tender and virile.

"This one is a little different.

"The one in Bermuda—there was no beginning and end of the days and nights for him. 'The world,' he had announced, 'can keep.'

"But this one. This one goes to bed at ten o'clock. What was it he said just last evening? 'Hey look, I'm a working man, honey. If I don't get my eight hours, I'm lost.'

"That man in Bermuda—you can't forget how he brought the tray of coffee and juice and English muffins to your bedside. Somehow he had awakened first and dressed swiftly and immaculately. That just couldn't be the one who, for three mornings now, has wailed, 'Honey, haven't you got the coffee ready, yet?'

"That man in Bermuda never ate—well, hardly ever. He just wanted to look at you. He lived on love.

"But this one. See him attack the hamburger. People look so *strange* when they eat, don't they?

"Who is this absolutely strange monster who shares the flat with you?

"Well, of course they are the same. The world has changed a little since Bermuda. And you might as well face it. You can't exactly go on forever on hot apple pie from Waterlot Inn and tropical moonlight. That lump over there in the corner of the bed, with his left ear sticking out of the covers, still asleep, is your man. Take a look at him. You might even walk over on tiptoe and kiss him on that ear.

"You might be the one to keep the tang of apple pie in the air of your apartment, even when there's no apple pie, and make the moonlight glow even in the middle of the day. It's just up to you. Keep on doing the little things he used to love, and maybe you'll make a sudden and breath-taking discovery. The lump over there might just be the man from Bermuda, after all. Keep your fingers crossed. And keep trying."

Candy's advice is the simple wisdom we all know best, and that is to be as feminine and loving as you can be, and your husband is sure to respond. It's fairly noticeable that a great many young women today —both single and married—regard their beauty as a kind of performance which is usually scheduled to go on at some other hour of the day. You see them going to school, at the supermarkets, at home, lounging around, unlovely and unkempt, burdened with hair curlers and deliberately unattractive clothes; and in the privacy of the bed-

room (clearly visible to the young husband, if the girl is married) adding even more artificiality to the edifice of allure. This is not to say that men don't like cosmetics, make-up, or beauty creams: in fact, they appreciate a girl who understands the needs and purposes of these beauty aids. But too many of them, on public display and in the semi-secrecy of the home, just can't help impressing on the man that beauty is something a bride purchases at the store. He may be proud of the "performance," at a party, or at dinner, or when meeting friends, but he'd much rather think that his own bride is beautiful always, in her own right. Bear that in mind at home, dear young brides. He thinks that you are beautiful, or he wouldn't have married you. That is your advantage. Just be sure that you do not lose it by striving for the wrong thing. Let me tell you this about a husband. Often he wakes up in the early morning while you are asleep and he looks at you long and lovingly. Be sure that it is you and not a display counter from the drugstore that he is looking at.

Who can advise the heart? Not many. But one way to the heart of a husband may be close to his meals, which he shares with you. It has often been observed that a sensible man rarely prefers a wife who is continually stirring a pot of gruel, sticking her head in the oven, and brushing her hair from her eyes with one hand while she pokes at a cake with a bit of straw with the other. He commends this loudly, and then runs off with a chorus girl some years later. A man likes a woman who has a way with cooking, and he becomes very proud of that. But the way need not be quantity, only quality.

Not as a course in cooking success, but as a first step—and only a small one—in that direction, let every young bride make one firm resolve. She will discover how to make a good cup of coffee, if that is all she ever learns to do. And here's how:

Of course, you will refrain from saying (or listening if anyone else says it) that "I'm not myself in the morning until I've had my cup of coffee." This is in itself grounds for desertion, as in Turkey at one time when a husband's refusal to give his wife a decent cup of coffee was considered sufficient grounds for divorce, if you'll pardon the expression. As for the drink itself, if you use cream, make it thick and heavy. Give your man a sizable cup or mug, preferably of his own choosing and not from your regular service. Then: start with a clean coffeemaker. Rinse coffeemaker with hot water before using. Wash thoroughly after each use. Rinse with hot water and dry. Fresh coffee is best. Buy coffee in the size can or package that will be used within a week after opening. Fresh water is important, too. Never use the first water out of the tap. Let it run a while.

Coffee should *never* be boiled. When coffee is boiled, an undesirable flavor change takes place.

Serve coffee as soon as possible after brewing. If necessary to let brewed coffee stand before serving, hold at serving temperature by placing the pot in a pan of hot water, or over very low heat on an asbestos pad.

The vacuum method: 1. Measure fresh cold water into lower bowl. Place on heat. 2. Place filter in upper bowl. Add measured amount of "fine grind" or "drip grind" coffee. 3. When water boils, reduce heat or turn off electricity. Then insert upper bowl into lower bowl. Twist to insure a tight seal. 4. Let most of water rise into upper bowl. Stir water and coffee thoroughly. In one to three minutes, remove from heat, exact time depending upon grind and strength desired. 5. When brew returns to lower bowl, remove upper bowl and coffee is ready to be served. 6. If a cloth filter is used, it should be thoroughly rinsed after each use (no soap) and kept immersed in cold water until used again.

Drip method: 1. Preheat pot by rinsing with hot water. 2. Measure "drip grind" coffee into filter section. 3. Measure fresh boiling water into upper container, and cover. 4. When dripping is completed, remove upper section. *Stir brew* to mix before serving.

Percolator method: 1. Measure fresh cold water into percolator. Place on heat until water boils. Remove from heat. 2. Measure regular grind coffee into basket. 3. Insert basket into percolator, return to heat, percolate slowly six to eight minutes. 4. Remove coffee basket and serve.

Steeped method: 1. Measure coffee into clean, scalded pot. 2. Bring freshly drawn water to a boil; pour over coffee; stir well. 3. Cover and let stand on an asbestos mat over low heat or in a warm place four to six minutes. 4. Strain.

In figuring out how much makes how many cups, the same proportions apply to all methods of making coffee. The basis is one Coffee

Brewing Institute standard measure of coffee and ¾ of a measuring cup (six fluid ounces) of water to yield approximately 5½ ounces of beverage. (A standard measure of coffee equals two level measuring tablespoons.)

And now, one last word to the wives. It is a tradition of fiction, the stage, movies, radio, and especially television, that the breakfast table is a scene of infinite significance to marital happiness. In a way it is. A wife should carefully scout, early in her honeymoon, what the chemistry seems to be between herself and her spouse before nine A.M.

In general, man being something of a happy and physical type of animal, he will arise with a bound, yodel happily in his shower, and approach his first cup of coffee with a display of optimism which may strike his wife as sheer idiocy. That is because most women are more of the nervous "night people" types than men. As the night wears on, a woman improves and improves, until she is normally quite scintillating at the hour when the male begins to wilt. Conversely, in the morning she awakes slowly and regretfully. She is a creature of claw and fang, filled with dark forebodings, quick to take offense and quicker to wound. Breakfast brings together a lout and a louse. Or if the chemistry of personality I have described is not quite in this balance, perhaps he is a bear and a boor, and she chirpy as a chickadee and a cricket.

Either way: watch, anticipate, avoid a clash.

One good way of doing this that I am going to suggest will surprise you. Civilized people are beginning to realize that the breakfast table is the most incendiary place to discuss bills, family, last night's party, or Mother's approaching visit. It is, however, a place where loving couples may eat in companionable and affectionate silence, and read the paper, or merely commune with the dark and secret stirrings within oneself, getting ready for the joys and perplexities of the day ahead. Good coffee is good. Silence, loving and not hateful, is good. The newspaper is good. Aimless chatter, half-settled disputes, and bad news are not good.

I suppose that no man ever is willing to convince himself of the truth concerning a woman and time. That fact is, of course, that women do not essentially believe in time. Time, to them, is a diamond watch, without hands. I can't tell whether or not this is a crime against nature, or the greatest accomplishment of civilization to date. My wife, for instance, sets and keeps all of the clocks in our house fifteen minutes fast, to counteract her tendency to be about fifteen minutes late all the time. This works out magnificently for her, believe it or not. She does everything according to these lying clocks, falls well behind them, tears off to catch a train or make an appointment, and is utterly charmed to find that she is precisely on time! I can't tell whether this is utter self-delusion or self-discipline. At first, I tried to counter this by subtracting the fifteen minutes from each of the clocks, but I soon discovered that subtracted time is not real time. You can't adjust to it. So I have solved the whole matter by having one clock on my desk which is set at the correct time, and I never look at any of the others.

But it would be ungallant of me to complain about the female attitude toward time, as it would be to point out that a husband, unlike all wives, is never quite able to comprehend that spending $20.00 for a hat marked down from $35.00 is inevitably regarded by the female not as a wise investment but as an actual *gain* of $15.00, which she is frequently apt to ask from her husband on the spot. No, I am more interested here in pointing out to a new bride the importance of timing, and how it relates to her husband.

Let me explain it this way. There is a phenomenon seen mostly in the suburbs known as the Catatonic Husband. He is, in fact, the victim of timing. What happens is about like this. He has had his shower and breakfast, and he is now driving—or being driven by his wife, a tableau I never could enjoy very much—to the station. What the wife should realize is that he is merely with her in body. The mind is well ahead of things at this point—he is already at the office, already wondering about this or that or trying to come to some decision about something that had been troubling him at closing time on the day before. At this moment, then, he fondly kisses his wife good-bye, glances up the track at the approaching train, grabs his briefcase, is half out of the car when his dreamboat says, musingly: "Old Man Haffenraffer stopped by the other day and looked at the retaining wall behind our house. He says if it isn't fixed right away the whole hill will come down on us. Our pipes need fixing, too. Mr. Scraggholder, the plumber, says that if we don't replace most of them, they'll burst from too much cloggage."

So you see the Catatonic Husband, half in, half out of his automobile. He stands there, transfixed, his mind racing. "Old Man Haffenraffer's pipes burst? The hill fell down on Mr. Scraggholder? What about the State contract at the office? Shall I take the next train . . . ?" At which point, his wife, having sown the seeds of destruction, blithely says: "Bye, honey. Have a good day," and drives away.

Yes. Timing. It's so important.

Another basic source of marital discord is the idea on the part of so many young brides that their chief mission in life is to do their man over, like a house. This arises in very many instances from the pure source of love—the wife sees her husband with affectionate eyes which perceive his better nature and his hidden talents. She wants to find a way to get these out of his private world and into the open where everyone else can see and admire. This much every loving wife will always try to do. Whether or not there is always a woman behind every successful man, there frequently is. She brings out the best in him, and often he succeeds only to please her, or because he knows that some of his lesser qualities, if too frequently revealed, will undo the high opinion she has of him. This is good for him.

But what a wife shouldn't do is to set out immediately to change his basic pattern. Let me explain. I'm not talking, I'm sure you know, about such things as getting him to pick up his socks off the floor, or to stop tossing his hat and coat all over the living room as soon as he's come into the house. Men are primarily creatures of action, and they'd *prefer* to drop the hat and coat on the nearest piece of furniture and get on immediately to the action, even if it turns out to be inaction. But in the long run, if your husband knows it irks you, he'll be willing enough to hang up his things, even if it strikes him, as it usually does, that putting a coat on a hanger is about the dullest and most domesticated task a real man can be called upon to perform. What I'm really talking about is a persistent and serious attempt to change his basic nature. The girl who has idolized her father, or perhaps even another man, and wants her husband to resemble this individual as closely as possible is most often the one who will attempt a transformation. This is a form of love, too, but to the recipient it can turn into a form of hostility which may endanger a marriage.

A wise girl will rarely pick her husband straight from his mother's apron strings. There is a time when a young male needs to get off by himself—away from the apron strings of his mother and before he's attached to a wife and find out things for himself, mostly about himself. If he's lucky enough to go to college, lucky enough to develop traits of his own during those four years instead of just running with the pack, he'll come out of it with some notion of what he considers good and bad in the world around him, in his own private life, and in his ways of adapting to the world. Thus, when he gets married, his character will have been formed to some degree. This is to the good— the girl can expect some consistency out of him in the years ahead, and she can evaluate the traits that she's going to be living with. She can expect to improve on the model somewhat. A husband will unconsciously expect counsel from his wife from the beginning, and, as he discovers over the years that her advice rarely fails him, he will cherish this side of his helpmate. But he doesn't want to be handed any book of rules. There are very few interfering mothers-in-law, despite the classic situation comedies shown so often in the movies and on TV, but they are directional forces in their daughters' lives (and they should be). It's an unhappy thing indeed if a young husband gets the idea (rightfully or wrongfully) that he's really taking orders from a higher-up through his wife.

The best plan for a girl is to move slowly in these matters. Let us hope and suppose that she hasn't married an old-maid type who is set into a pattern of little ways which are necessary to keep him happy. But let us suppose that her man has at least developed some tastes of his own. Let the wife play it cool for a time, I suggest, and find these out. They may be small things which seem large to him, or large things which *are* large. Well, here are some that a wife should look out for.

The male animal, unless he is incurably adolescent, does not run in a herd all his life. If he has lived in a dorm of fraternity house at college, or teamed up with a couple of his friends to share an apartment during the early years of his business career, it is natural for him to want a place of his own. This life in his own diggings develops in him, not a dog in the manger attitude—that is not what I am getting at—but an intense enjoyment of periods when he is absolutely alone. He plays the music he wants, as loud as he wants, and as long as he wants. He gets a little drunk if he feels like it. He has dinner at midnight, or none at all. He reads in the bathtub for hours, refreshed by a battery of scotches-and-soda set up on the rim of the tub. He goes out and walks all Friday night and sleeps all day Saturday. Pure unadulterated selfishness—right! But he begins to understand the pure joy of privacy as he indulges in these sybaritic impurities. That is one of a man's most important needs, and a wife—even a newlywed—should recognize it. The first glories of wedded life are going to keep him at your side through every second of the day and night. But in time, that need for privacy will assert itself, and a good thing it will be for both of you.

Many modern homes adapt as an architectural principle the barnyard theory that everything should be done in proximity to everyone, and thus, with the door becoming practically obsolete, living is reduced to one long predictable bore. Keep the doors in your life, is my word to the wives. Let your man retire to his room, if he is lucky enough to have one, or step outdoors for a walk, or read the newspaper or a book, or do his work, without feeling that by so doing he is relegating you to second place in his life.

I have observed that in a great many U.S. homes the father is known as an individual who likes to fuddy-duddy around in the bathroom, and that once in, it will take hours to dislodge him. This is frequently the case, and true enough except for the fuddy-duddy part of it. The real explanation is that this is the one spot where a man can shut the door and be alone for a period of time, with his thoughts or with no thoughts, if he chooses. Young lady, be sure to give him some time to himself. He will love you more, not less, for it.

That "no thoughts" up there is another key point. Women are usually, in contrast to men, the thoroughbred type, nervous, full of plans and fears and joys, continually smelling smoke somewhere, hearing burglars everywhere, and always working toward the millennium, which should be achieved, if possible, by tomorrow at the earliest. Men, on the contrary, rarely throw off at any time in their lives a small-boy habit—the same one which a cat often achieves by simple self hypnosis—of doing nothing at all. You will often come upon him sitting in his chair, leaning on a fence, or gazing, unseeing, at some undistinguished object. This does not mean that he is ill, or that he is overcome by some great grief, or sunk in the contemplation of some grand design. He is merely in a state of being. He is resting his mind, letting his metabolism catch up a little, giving his nerves a chance to unhitch from the director's switchboard and allowing the follicles of the hair to settle more comfortably into their appointed tasks. Let him be. In a minute or two he will snap out of it and be a very bear of energy, rearing about to get things done. Enjoy his brief absences from reality—*he* does.

There are some things which were part of his bachelor life, which, of course, must be omitted from the married state. You have every right to expect and demand that he quit hanging out with the boys at the poolroom, the drugstore, or the club, at least to the degree that he used to. I knew of one young husband, now happily bereft of the habit, who actually did go down to the corner drugstore and watch the girls go by—meanwhile leaving his wife at home with their infant. All he needed was a spanking which he ultimately delivered to himself. But every young wife should know that male companionship—and not on double dates either—is a necessity of every man's existence, in proper proportion to his home responsibilities. You've observed the pattern, perhaps, at the cocktail parties of young marrieds and their older counterparts. After the first greetings are over, the men drift out into the kitchen, and the women occupy the living room, all of them talking pleasantly enough and enjoying their drinks. It isn't because the men necessarily want to tell off-color stories (their wives undoubtedly know stronger ones) or sit on the edge of a sink instead of a sofa. The fact is, that they want to chew the fat a little bit with members of their own sex exclusively. Most men do not remember their years in military service with undiluted joy. But one of the things they will admit to enjoying was the male companionship. True, most of it was devoted to talking about the girls and trying to get away to see them. But in retrospect, the service had its merits and, in time, men even will admit to having enjoyed parts of their tour of duty.

So, let him get out with the boys from time to time. Most young men have athletic habits—tennis, golf, swimming, squash, or just fooling around a gym—which are abruptly cut off by marriage. Don't believe, unless you are actually a whiz at sports and can really keep up with him, that his sets, rounds or games with you are a fair substitute for the fierce fires of competition against a man of his own athletic skills. I personally am not very much for nights spent boozing with the boys or losing the family bankroll at a game of poker, and I suggest that any sensible girl try to soft-pedal these sessions—although not *forbid* them—for the sake of encouraging the husband in a continuance of his athletic pursuits. After all, these are good for his body and spirit and, over the years, the total number of hours devoted to them will diminish. But it's another facet of the male animal a young wife does well to keep in mind.

And lastly, about old girl friends. This is another holdover from bachelor life which will diminish pleasantly as the years go on, as his former glamor girls turn into plump matrons and mothers of broods of children. But in the beginning of your life together, you are sure to learn the names of certain other young ladies who will become part of your world, as they are part of his remembrances. Your husband gallantly will assure you that they were merely friends, but they will pop up so unexpectedly—even to *him*—and so often in his conversation, that it may occur to you that this is carrying friendship to the extreme. My advice is, forget it. Search your own heart. Realize that you have many male friends who have been good and even dear to you in your life, and you would think it strange and entirely uncalled for if your husband flew into a rage every time their names were mentioned. Don't worry—you'll mention them enough to annoy him, as it is. And I can predict at least a fight or two, entirely without any justice to it on either side, on this very question. These old girl friends, being females, may write to him, meet him accidentally on the street, or even telephone the house when they know you are there—so insatiable are they for the merest hint as to how he feels about his married state. Bear with this—your husband is only amused by it. Remember, he chose *you.*

One of the penalties about being so cool and such a good sport about it all is that you may be called upon some time to entertain the old girl friend in company with her latest date, or perhaps her latest husband. Under these circumstances, she will appear in as ravishing a costume as the laws of decency will permit, will flounce around *your* home like Carmen with a rose in her teeth, and will stick to your husband like a leech, monopolizing him and driving him into a state of ecstasy by reminiscences of the great, wild, old times they had together. Meanwhile, you will be saddled with the other man, a chap with an extremely low state of vitality, whose conversation centers around the weather, his mother's recent operation, and his job —something having to do with hardware inventories.

Take it easy. Do not engage in any feline controversies with your erstwhile rival, or mention to your husband after she and her date have finally gone, that he seemed to laugh too gaily at her sallies. Just be above it all, and be your own charming self. Don't overdo it, but give your husband a chance to make the same comparison he's already made. This may be the greatest evening you've ever had with him, from his admiring point of view. Have faith in your husband—and keep your eye on *her*.

A lesser thorn in your marital side will be the gradually extending web of female acquaintances your husband will make in his working hours. They have certain advantages on you, it will seem. He sees some of them, a secretary, for instance, from six to eight hours daily. He may even lunch with some of these people, or have a drink with them for business reasons after work. This is all normal. It is also normal for him to mention them in his evening conversations, to tell little anecdotes concerning their wit or the lack of it, and probably to describe the more attractive girls in more attractive terms than they deserve. Don't pay any attention to this. This to your husband is all part of his job. These are the furniture of his office world as much as his desk and the water-cooler are. They become devilishly familiar to him, in time, but they are not familiar in the wrong sense unless he is an absolute fool, which we will assume that he is not. Take it calmly: home is where the heart is. The best part of him is all yours.

And while I am about the business end of it, may I mention a few mistakes that some of the girls commit, and probably never know they do? Let me put it in the form of a few suggestions:

1. Try to keep telephone calls to him at the office to a minimum. If you must reach him during office hours, be brief and to the point. Don't expect too many calls per day from him (some office managers forbid this altogether or make their employees register personal calls). And don't expect any highly personal responses from him, since he may be seated with someone within earshot of his replies, and then, too, there is also the office switchboard, which has access to whatever you are saying, whether accidentally or otherwise. It follows that if you have something of a personal nature to discuss and if it can wait even a few minutes, ask him to call you back when he's relatively free. If it's a crisis that can wait, don't toss it to him at all while he's working. It might be very damaging to something vital he's just in the midst of working out.

2. When you *do* call the office, remember at all times that although there may be people there who have some obligations to him—such as a secretary or a switchboard operator or an office associate—they don't owe you a thing, and their helpfulness is pure courtesy and not a requirement.

3. If your husband has anyone working for him, they do not work for you and should not be expected to carry out any errands. If they do, the errands should be regarded as personal favors and requested at points few and far between.

4. Never appear at the office at all, even if your husband asks you to. There are obvious exceptions to this, in the case of necessity. But the rule should apply generally, whether your husband is just starting at the bottom of the ladder, or is the boss. The reasons for this are not at all uncomplimentary to you: they are simply based on hard common sense.

Amen.

Wife-lines: To a new husband

I would like first to make some suggestions as to the furnishing of your new home, and then—as Mr. F.A.B. has already addressed some sage, and perhaps prejudiced, counsel to the new bride—I should like to take my turn in addressing myself personally to the new husband and head of the house. But, first, to these other practical matter:

CREATING A NEW HOME

Blessings abide with the bride and groom who start out with a sound plan and budget for outfitting their new home. The unison they achieve augurs happily for what lies ahead of them. The chances are that a bride herself will wish to select furnishings as carefully as she has chosen her husband, and to do it wisely she must have a program. Bride and groom by working together for visual harmony in the appointments and decor of their new home create a background that reflects their inner harmony and mutual happiness. That choice, in partnership of things that blend perfectly, will form a setting in which to enjoy their guests and each other.

Fat, and sometimes tiresome, books have been written about the vast, comparatively uncharted sea of interior decoration, some of it good, a great deal of it of no use to anybody. Set down here is a brief outline of what is fundamental in a new home.

AS TO FURNITURE

The first abode of a bride and groom today is likely to be two or three rooms and a kitchen, unless they are able, as sometimes happens, to move into a house that they will live in for some years to come. As this is not the happy circumstance of most brides, it is the basic furniture and background of a small apartment that receives first attention of any young couple. And this is the place to state that all fundamental pieces should be first-rate. Whether those pieces will be contemporary or traditional in type, it is comforting to know that modern and traditional pieces live agreeably together, for the time will come when changing tastes will dictate this forced relationship.

A big comfortable sofa of club type is fundamental. It may be of the Lawson style, or a sectional piece of modern design, or a pair of small sofas each of which will seat two people without crowding. Next "must" selection is a lounge chair. These upholstered pieces should be the best one can afford, for they will go through life with the new family and accommodate themselves to any future home it may have, simple or grand. They will need reupholstering and rewebbing from time to time through the years, but they will always be an important part of the household.

Hardwood pieces built on simple lines may be "budget" priced because they may be replaced with finer pieces as a home develops. A well-built piece, good-looking and practical, may some day go to a less important room than the living room, and may be replaced by a finer one that squares with a rising income and more ambitious decorating ideas. Upholstered pieces, however, bought at the start go on forever if they are good.

Without fail, have a budget for furnishings and be cold-blooded in allotting money to its items. First call after the upholstered living-

room pieces is for the best box springs and mattresses that one can afford. They take the brunt of the living, and their life is endless. *Note:* If the first home is but one room with perhaps a kitchen and dining foyer, and upholstered pieces must be sat upon as well as slept on, the excellent combination of two studio couches with a square table in the corner, making a good-looking unit, is recommended. It fulfills both functions capably. Both pieces may be later moved decorously into other and more spacious surroundings.

Investment in good reproduction pieces of furniture pays. They are not cheap, but they endure. Where the budget is generous, buy them because they grow more valuable through the years.

To the list of furniture for a combined living and dining room, to the fundamental upholstered pieces, should be added a table that seats four at least. It will serve for dining or buffet or bar, or as a card table. It should be flanked by a pair of straight chairs with upholstered or perhaps rush seats. A coffee table, twenty-eight inches square between a pair of love seats, or in front of a sofa if a sofa has been decided upon, has a maximum of utility and appearance. A game table for gin rummy, backgammon, or bridge will serve as a lamp table when not on active duty. When you select a radio, whether combined with television or record player, keep to simple lines so that it will not clash with furniture in the room, nor with what may be bought later. A sound wall, which may include shelving for books, a record player, and television or radio is a sightly and useful unit for a well-used living room.

If there is no fireplace, the focus of interest in a room can be a large sofa with a pair of lounge chairs. This combination recurs over and over again in simple or elaborate homes, and it recurs for the very good reason that this combination is eminently practical. Additional importance to this grouping may be lent by hanging above the sofa a large sheet mirror, flush with the wall, or a big picture which may be a reproduction, or a grouping of pictures. These may be old silhouettes, flower or fashion prints, or game-bird or sporting prints, or perhaps a collection of old Chinese prints. Arrangements of small objects of kindred type may be used, as a group of masks or primitive sculptures. Lamps in a living room should serve a dual purpose—to furnish light for reading and soft light for conversation when there are guests. For this purpose two-light lamps fitted with a strong bulb and one of lower power are a practical answer.

AS TO FABRICS

In selecting fabrics to cover furniture, literally any fabric may be chosen provided it is firmly woven. Texture fabrics, tweeds, and even sailcloth have all been used with inspiring results by clever decorators, including brides themselves. Glazed or unglazed chintzes in simple or formal patterns, in accord with cottage furnishings or period decor, are effective and improve with age. Formal satins and brocades are most at home in stately surroundings, though satin may often be muted to modest surroundings if the furniture is elegant in line and built of fine woods. Fabrics, so important a part of the decorative scheme of any home, must be selected with consideration for all elements making up that home: its size, the woods, and the formality or informality of the life to be lived within it. Care in this department will pay pyramiding dividends in the pleasure they will give through the years.

A good rule to keep in mind in buying curtains is that sheer glass curtains should be triple the window width so that they fall in generous folds. And finally, do not pick out a more expensive fabric in order to slit it because that will cheapen the fabric and you will not get the effect you hoped for. Inexpensive materials generously used will produce a richer and more luxurious result than expensive fabrics used scantily. This is the one instance when half a loaf is worse than none at all.

AS TO CARPETS

Carpet, wall to wall, makes a room look larger, more luxurious. On a budget, cotton carpeting in any "decorator" or standard color comes in broadloom widths, and over a carpet felt it makes a sturdy and effective floor covering. More expensive broadloom carpeting, when used wall to wall in a first home, is also practical when it falls within budgetary limits, since when it is transferred to a later home it may be bound to make a handsome rug where hardwood floors make a satisfactory border.

When one is putting a room together, it is of first importance that pieces are scaled to the size of the room and the height of the ceiling. There should be no mammoth, overstuffed pieces in a smallish room or a towering breakfront where ceilings are low, nor, for that matter, pieces too small for a big room with high ceilings. Fortunately, designers today have scaled furniture of all sorts to suit rooms in modern houses and apartments.

A double headboard for twin beds is both practical and decoratively sound. The two beds, set side by side to look like one when covered with a counterpane, make for greater unity and give an effect of greater spaciousness to the room. It is not essential for twin bedside tables to be set beside the beds. Often a pair of low two- or three-drawer chests to hold bedside lamps is practical; they provide storage for small clutter and are often convenient to have near a bed.

AS TO COLORS

Color is one of the hardest things to discuss. In approaching it, it is pertinent to speak of a common mistake, that of choosing too light a shade of the color you have selected. For day-to-day living, it will be found that a middle value—that is, a middle value of the color chosen —will make a room more attractive and livable, and form a better background for furniture. Nearly always it is a good rule to have all woodwork, baseboards, window trim, and doors painted the same color as the walls. In planning a color scheme, the old decorator trick of using a favorite piece of fine porcelain or faïence, a picture or a piece of beautiful fabric, as a starting point in plotting the color scheme is as solid as twenty-four-carat gold.

AS TO WIVES

My husband has written some "words to the wives" in the foregoing pages which might make it seem that he has one of the most irritating and least understanding spouses in the whole world, but fortunately close at hand to provide for his research. My only defense is that he is a very observing man, and, of course, the countryside is teeming with other marriages to observe and husbands and wives to interview. I hope I have not been too productive a case history. But here is my chance to get back at him and draw a black picture of an impossible husband and his heartrending ways.

I wouldn't—and couldn't, in fact—do that. But there are a great many ways, large and small, in which a husband can make his wife's life easier. I shall try to touch on them with the feeling that if a young man is warned in advance he can take his course of action on the basis of thought and decision rather than just a snap judgment.

Perhaps it is "just like a woman" to talk about money first. But you are going to be discussing money for a long time to come. One of your first pronouncements to yourself as a young husband should be that you will never, *never,* let money be the cause of a disagreement involving any strong emotional outbursts. Money will make you glad, and it will make you sad, many, many times during your life. But it will always be there as a day-to-day problem that must be faced, so you might as well decide at the beginning that it will be regarded as objectively as possible. Save your emotions for the meaningful things in life. Money is a tool you will need, but no more.

The most important first move is to open a bank account. You and your wife probably have had your own accounts in the past, so what I'll say next may seem superfluous, but I'll say it anyway, like a woman. Cashing your weekly salary check and then expecting to make it spread out until the next check appears, with all obligations taken care of, just isn't going to work at all. Human nature expands in a well known way to the bulge of a relatively large wad of bills in the wallet, and you'll find that you've dropped into a routine of overspending in the few days (or hours) after you've been paid, and starving in the last hours (or days) before the next pay check comes along.

But more than that, a checking account at a bank establishes your credit in amazing ways. I'll never forget the lesson a little storekeeper once taught me about credit. In those days I paid cash for everything on the theory that this made me a customer who was all paid up and hence the more desirable. But one time, discovering I had forgotten my purse, I had to tell the storekeeper that I would cancel my order, and come back another time when I could pay him in cash. He urged me to open a charge account: "How can I tell if you're honest if we don't try it out and see?" he asked. I soon found that a charge account left me with more cash for my other needs. Of course, it's a well-known fact that the more charge accounts the greater the temptation to overspend, and that might be the reason why merchants prefer them. But mostly I believe that they feel the charge account encourages consistent purchasing in their store and builds up a relationship of trust between merchant and customer. I for one am a defender of our credit age. Too many times over the years, I have been compelled to pass up bargains or actual necessities because of a lack of immediate funds. Getting the money later on won't help in the crisis.

So I say establish your credit by making a good banking connection. And then, in the event of any financial problems, you will have as an adviser one of the bank executives and a firm basis on which to make loans should the need arise.

Now, what kind of account should you have? Let me go on record against the joint checking account. Husbands are usually pretty good with banking problems and figures, but let us face the fact that wives, and particularly young ones, are not very adept at it. The joint checking account seems at first to be the most loving arrangement—each has access to the family money. But that only runs into the most horrifying messes as the total amount of money in the bank at any given time is subject to simultaneous writing of checks by both parties, and frequent omissions and forgettings (I am sorry to say) by the wife in keeping her end of the account straight. As a result, the young couple rarely knows where it stands. One of the first things to learn about any checking account is that when you get a statement from the bank and look at the total it does not represent what you now have, but only the total at the time of drawing up the statement. Meanwhile, if you have written many or few checks, you must total these carefully and accurately and subtract this sum from the statement total before you come to a clear figure of what money you actually have available.

I suggest three kinds of accounts. The "regular checking account" usually requires a minimum figure in the bank at all times, and perhaps this figure is too substantial as a starter for you to establish. But do so as soon as you can. The regular checking account is the key to all of your credit arrangements, and guarantees your acceptance under all sorts of financial situations at home and particularly when you are out of town. The "special checking account," with no minimum balance required, does not carry the same kind of credit assurance, but it may be more sensible for you at the outset, even with its cost of ten cents a check. Ideally, I would recommend that the husband maintain a regular checking account. Then, the wife has her own special checking account, as well. The family uses the regular account for the paying of sizable bills such as rent, installments on the car, insurance, and the like. The special checking account is for the wife's household— expenditures: food, laundry, clothes, etc. Then, there should be a savings account, which earns interest, into which regular amounts are deposited for a "baby fund," a "house fund," a "trip to Europe" fund, or other projects of your happy future. These three seem to work out the best for the young family. If the husband finds he cannot swing a regular checking account to begin with, he should start out with a special checking account of his own.

Bankers can never understand how non-bankers can mess up a perfectly simple process like keeping checking records straight, but it can be done. Having two accounts is one of the best answers to the confusions of an only hazily estimated total-in-account, and the terrible embarrassments of a check that bounces. You simply let one of the accounts lie fallow, in time of doubt, and use the one closest to the actual figures to avoid any distressing experiences. You'll see that I'm right—more than once you'll be glad, sir, to turn to your wife's account, or help her out with some of your checks when the mists rise around the totals and a check becomes not a piece of monetary exchange but a question mark.

Now, as to budgeting. This is one of the most misunderstood subjects in the world, and one of the most miserable, as well, if you want my real opinion. I know families where the husband or wife keeps a strict budget and the members are put on such a strict allowance that they have to come whining to each other for cab or liquor money, genuflecting when the funds are squeezed out of the budget with a stern warning. This is a living death, making such a fetish out of security. But the opposite can be almost as bad, and perhaps worse. So my suggestion is that a young husband should draw up a budget just to see what the natural limitations of spending should be and then use the budget as a guide rather than an instrument of torture. Budgets are not made to be disregarded—but almost so.

One of the first things you should do about a budget is to decide upon the direction you think that your lives will take together. Young people have different ideas. Some don't care how they live if they can get in plenty of weekend skiing; others get more out of a car as a status symbol than a home; others need a week-end hideaway more than anything in life, and are willing to bypass much else to get it. Most of us want all of these things, but some will predominate more than others. That's why you should know in advance where your real preferences fall. Don't sink all your money in an expensive apartment at some swank address if your friends, and you most of all, aren't going to get real and continuing pleasure out of living there.

However, let's get down to brass tacks. Here is a budget which is worked out in percentage points of your take-home pay. Let's assume that your taxes have been withheld and that the amount, by and large, will be what your final tax should be, since that's the general purpose behind these fixed figures, to begin with. Then, here is how you can break down the resulting take-home figure as to probable monthly expenditures.

HOUSING	29.0%
FOOD	20.5%
CLOTHES	10.0%
ENTERTAINMENT	9.0%
MEDICAL	4.5%
INSURANCE	4.5%
TRANSPORTATION	9.0%
SAVINGS	6.0%
OTHER	7.5%

I must repeat, of course, that this is only for general guidance. After a little experience you may be able to discover areas where you are overspending regularly or saving consistently, and you can make an adjustment according to your own particular habits of expenditure.

Perhaps superfluously, I must suggest that the young husband look on three things with a mature—and what may seem to him too mature —eye. They are hospitalization, insurance, and a will. Hospitalization, family style, is a must today, for accidents as well as for the babies ahead. Do it now, if you are not already a member through your business. And sign up for "the works." The high cost of being sick today brings its own kind of sinking feeling with it. So be prepared. The virtues of insurance have been pointed out so often, and some of its defects, that we needn't go into it in detail. But just let's look at it one way. You are mortal—every time you cross a street, eat a meal or draw a breath (boy, am I a crepe-hanger!) may be the last time in this vale of tears. Yes, I know that at your age you feel immortal, and I, too, expect to live to be at least ninety-nine, as my grandfather did. But it is an act of love toward your wife to have at least enough life insurance to enable her to meet any and all financial obligations if you are suddenly removed from the scene—and a will to confirm who gets what. As you grow older, these will become necessities rather than wise precautions, so why not start out with them at the outset?

Before we get away from money, which I am sure you are going to earn in abundance (most wives, you must know, really only hope that their husbands will earn just what is needed for their mutual happiness), let me say something about where parents fit into this scheme. The total income of a newly wedded couple strikes most parents as being adequate for a brace of not too demanding white mice and they are apt to try and supplement this with gifts for the house, clothing for their daughter, and other gestures meant to lighten the load at the beginning. Young sir, do not get on your high horse and breathe fire at the very thought that someone might be thoughtful enough to give you a helping hand. No one expects that you are going to be the kind of leech who will start out a "home" completely subsidized by your own or your wife's parents—yet on the other end of the scale, unless you are extraordinarily gifted in the art of being successful and making money, no one is going to suppose that you can provide everything needed on all sides, at least for some time to come. If a little help is offered, take it in the same spirit in which it is given—that is, one part of the family helping another.

Here we are at in-laws, already. About the best advice I can give a young husband on the subject of his in-laws is to accept them calmly as part of the natural foliage of the region, inevitable as gravity, but not really bad when you get used to them.

The underlying relationship between a girl and her parents is not always understood by her new husband. Being a man, he is delighted to be away from his own family. He has probably been away from them for some time already, and he is willing to listen to all of their advice and then probably disregard it in a gesture of sheer masculine individuality. Acting on what he knows about his own feelings, the young husband often considers that he has done his wife a great favor by removing her from such obviously mediocre surroundings and placing her in juxtaposition with the wonders of life with him. He is only half right in so thinking. Life *is* full of wonders with him. But a girl doesn't usually look upon marriage as an escape from home, although I suppose some exceptions do. She looks upon it as way of expanding her own existence, and she expects to keep up a very close relationship with her parents. It should be said in their favor that generally the parents of the bride usually approve of the groom, (with certain misgivings, perhaps, which they try not to show). The father of the groom usually is the least problem of all, and views the entire situation with a knowing and slightly amused detachment. The mother of the groom is usually the most highly charged, emotionally, of the whole group. It is her natural instinct to consider the bride as a rival for her son's affections, and a successful one. Most young brides find a way to cope with this, but the groom should help by preventing *his* mother from indulging too much in the affairs of the new household. He is apt to look indulgently upon her efforts, and rightfully so, since they are well intentioned. But he must realize that a girl is already accustomed to following the advice of her own parents, and it should not surprise him to find her favoring their suggestions over those from his side of the family.

Therefore, the groom should realize that the bond between a girl and her mother is not automatically severed by marriage. On the contrary, it is actually strengthened by the very fact of marriage. He will find that whereas before he was arrayed against a mother and daughter, he is now faced by two women, a far more formidable combination.

The whole situation, however, appears to be far more complicated than it actually is. Good humor, sir, and a little of the affection you hold for your wife beamed in the direction of her parents will do wonders under most situations. The other answers are to be found in pure geography. Don't live too near either of your in-laws if you can arrange it, and don't live *with* them by any means.

My husband has mentioned "timing" in his word to the wives. That works both ways, of course, as do so many of the things we have been discussing here. Men are thoroughly indoctrinated in the inalienable rights of women to perform all of the sewing, ironing, and cleaning chores around the house. I don't mind that at all, even though I must observe in passing that men (such as my husband) who can do these things, actually do them better than women. They just don't *want* to do them, which I think is O.K. too. But here is where timing is of such importance. Let's set the scene. The couple is dressing for a party. The wife, as usual, is minutes behind on her schedule. She knows that if she doesn't keep up at her present breakneck speed the moment is sure to come when her husband, after prowling the house like a wounded lion, will stick his head in the bedroom and ask: "Aren't you ready, *yet?*" The implication is, of course, that well disciplined preparation could have speeded up things a little. And it is usually at this critical beforehand point that the husband appears with a shirt or other garment in his hand and, with the look of a small boy announcing the demise of his favorite frog, announces: "There's a button missing." The Keeper of the Buttons is expected, of course, to drop everything at this point and repair the damage immediately and in high good humor. Please, young sir, when this moment pops into your life, pop back into your shirt supply and find a substitute with all the buttons on deck. Or, if you're a one-dress-shirt man, check it over a day or so in advance. That's the kind of "timing" a wife really can appreciate.

I would say that one of the most important rules of marriage is to keep such differences as you are going to have always on the private side. This extends to all ends of the spectrum. I mean that a continuing attitude of criticism of your wife in public can be just as bad as giving her a good tongue-lashing. I have observed a couple over the years who originally indulged in a kind of affectionate belittlement of the other as a sort of a social game. It wasn't long before the belittlement became a habit and the affectionate attitude was dropped. The couple wound up spending most of their conversational time in public sniping at each other and accomplished little more than exposing their numerous faults to all of their friends. The result of this is far sadder than if they had been having hot arguments all this time. So, stand up for your wife in front of others. It does not become you as a man to criticize her. Don't be afraid to treat her with admiration and affection: a small gesture or words of support mean a great deal to a girl in front of others. We are supposed to be emancipated, we have our own careers, we wear levis and sweatshirts just like the boys, drive the cars, and do many things we've always been dying to do. But we still are feminine enough to get a thrill out of a man who will hold a car door open for us, or rise to his feet when ladies enter a room. Maybe we're wrong about this; maybe we want to have our cake and eat it, too, and it's all our own fault. But won't you let us cling to some of the feminine things, too? Because a woman in her heart really reveres a true man, who is gentle because he is strong. This world is so full of males who are not "men," just boys grown old. Manhood, it would seem, is not a gift of time, but something which must be achieved. There is nothing quite like it, gentlemen, in our opinions. A man, at any age, is a wondrous thing, and when we find a *young* man—there you have the finest thing on earth. So please be that man, and your marriage will always flourish.

I have actually heard one husband grind his teeth on the way home after work and growl: "Now, I have to 'entertain' my wife." I think he had the wrong idea. A wife always looks forward to rejoining her husband at the end of the day, but it is to be with him, not to be "entertained." I would say that this husband was somewhere near the truth, but on the unhappier side of it. Wives don't need entertainment, but they do need change. A husband will usually confess that there are aspects of his job which are enjoyable—friendships, challenges, successes, a continuing broadening process as his career develops. That is not to say that his job is just a little joy, but it is somewhat more interesting than housewifely chores. When he comes home at night he is tired and home is his haven. He wants to stretch out, rest, and unwind. At this point no wife is going to ask to be taken out for dinner or to be entertained. But I believe that a husband should realize that even living in a mansion continually can be boring, and boredom quickly can turn into a kind of mental fatigue. Plan on giving her a "change of pace" with fair regularity. It can be as simple as a walk in the woods, or a picnic over the weekend, or a drive to a newly discovered country inn. It can be just a movie on a weekday night, or a chance to meet you in town for a drink at a favorite bar. It isn't that she needs a lot of money spent on her, you see. It's a change of pace that she needs most. At least once a month, you should plan a really important date to do something that you wouldn't ordinarily do, and save ahead for the extra expenses this will probably involve. These expeditions are really fun and preserve the joys of your courting days. A weekend at a modest resort, a trip out of town to attend some exciting sports event, a visit to a part of the country you've never seen before, or merely a meal at a fabulous restaurant can be a great adventure.

There are many other things I *could* say here but won't because all the wisdom concerning marriage is, after all, based upon one thing and one thing only. Isn't it curious that so wise and deeply meaningful an insight should have been made by a man as complicated and sad as Oscar Wilde? Yet, of all the things ever said about wives, I commend this to you: *"Women are meant to be loved, not to be understood."*

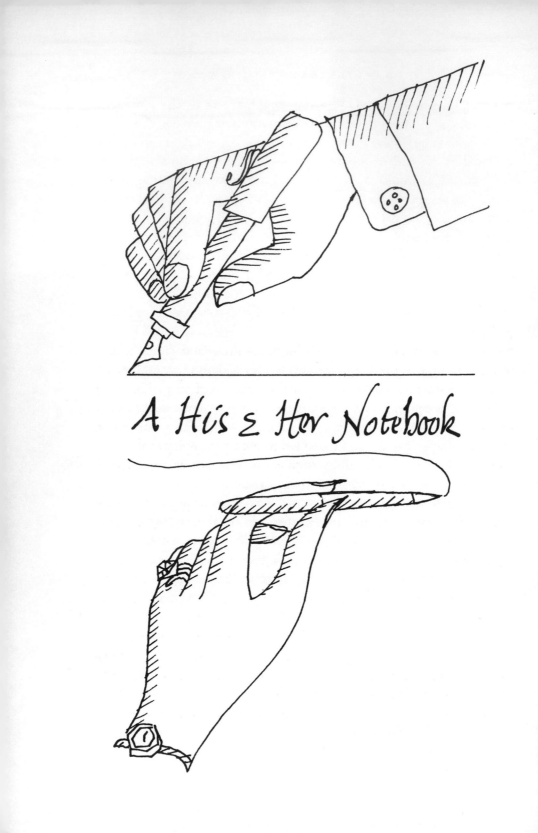

A His & Her Notebook

Chapter Five

🌹

A His & Her Notebook

And so, on to the happy anniversaries

ONE OF THE GREATEST things about marriage, and one that is wholly incomprehensible to newlyweds, is that the right marriage increases in happiness as the years roll by. It seems to them, at first, that nothing in the world could be an improvement on their present state of bliss. But with the problems and pleasures of the years, something even more beautiful takes form, and each anniversary marks this ever more clearly. So do not look down, young newlyweds, on these future signposts: they are the marks of your life ahead.

The traditional anniversaries are as follows: 1st, paper; 2nd, cotton; 3rd, leather; 4th, fruit and flowers, silk; 5th, wooden; 6th, sugar and candy, iron; 7th, woolen or copper; 8th, bronze or pottery; 9th, willowware or pottery; 10th, tin or aluminum; 11th, steel; 12th, silk or linen; 13th, lace; 14th, ivory, 15th, crystal; 20th, china; 25th, silver; 30th, pearl; 35th, coral; 40th, ruby; 45th, sapphire; 50th, golden; 55th, emerald; 60th and 75th, diamond.

Now, in an expanding world these traditional anniversaries have seemed to some to lack scope, so various helpful groups have banded together to cover a little more ground. The Jewelry Industry Council and the Retail Jewelers of America, Inc., aided and abetted by the National Wholesale Jewelers Association, all gentlemen who look

kindly on the institution of marriage, have released an official list, which goes as follows:

1st, clocks; 2d, china; 3rd, crystal and glass; 4th, electrical appliances; 5th, silverware; 6th, wood; 7th, desk, pen and pencil sets; 8th, linens and laces; 9th, leather; 10th, diamond jewelry; 11th, fashion jewelry, accessories; 12th, pearls or colored gems; 13th, textiles, furs; 14th, gold jewelry; 15th, watches; 16th, silver hollow ware; 17th, furniture; 18th, porcelain; 19th, bronze; 20th, platinum; 25th, sterling, silver jubilee; 30th, diamond; 35th, jade; 40th, ruby; 45th, sapphire; 50th, golden jubilee; 55th, emerald; 60th, diamond jubilee.

Keep thy eyes wide open before marriage,
and half shut afterwards.

BENJAMIN FRANKLIN

Record of Wedding Guests

Record of Wedding Guests

Record of Wedding Guests

_____

_____

_____

_____

_____

_____

_____

_____

_____

_____

_____

_____

_____

_____

Record of Wedding Guests

❧ GIFT RECORD ❧

Name & Address	Description	Acknowl.

GIFT RECORD

Name & Address	Description	Acknowl.

GIFT RECORD

Name & Address	Description	Acknowl.

⸗❧{ GIFT RECORD }❧⸗

Name & Address	Description	Acknowl.

Index

DATE DUE

VERMONT S. COLLEGE
MONTPELIER, VT.